The Lost

Passions of Jesus

The Lost
Passions of Jesus

Donald L. Milam, Jr.
with Classic Writings from History

Mercy Place

Distributed by
Destiny Image® Publishers, Inc.
P.O. Box 310
Shippensburg, PA 17257-0310

ISBN 0-9677402-0-7

For Worldwide Distribution
Printed in the U.S.A.

3 4 5 6 7 8 9 10 11 12 13 / 10 09 08 07 06 05

This book and all other Destiny Image, Revival Press, Mercy Place, Fresh Bread, and Treasure House books are available at Christian bookstores and distributors worldwide.

For a U.S. bookstore nearest you, call **1-800-722-6774**.
For more information on foreign distributors, call **717-532-3040**.
Or reach us on the Internet: **http://www.destinyimage.com**

Dedication

THIS BOOK IS DEDICATED to the hundreds
the world in whom the flame of passion has bee
of you were once vitally involved in the purposes of
with passion and zeal for our Lord and thought that y
ference in the Body of Christ. Time began to wear off
sionate zeal. Unfulfilled expectations, hurt and
disappointment, personal failure, and finally disillusic
marks on your soul. The end result was that many of y
your hopes and dreams or still stayed in the Church,
tration.

I understand your pain and your discouragemen
the midst of your world, having abandoned my own ho
Church and ultimately my Lord. Everything changed
five and a half years ago when, in the middle of my sle
ing me back with this question, "Why are you robbing

Allow me to lovingly declare to you that this is the
is reaching out to "prodigals" around the globe and wo
His arms. His desire is to rekindle in you the flame of

It is my prayer that this book will find its way into
of these prodigals and that its words will rebirth a ne
and our God.

Acknowledgments

I WOULD LIKE TO ACKNOWLEDGE the following people who have had an impact on the rediscovery in my life of the passions of the Lord Jesus.

My father, Don Milam, Sr., who first introduced me to the Lord.

Don and Cathy Nori, who have been faithful friends and a great encouragement in my journey. Don, your passion for the Most Holy Place has been a great inspiration to me.

Kim and Becky Hayfield, our wonderful friends for more than 20 years. You have taught us much on hearing the voice of the Lord.

My grown children and their spouses, Kelly and Ron, Andy and Marcy, and Jeff, whom I love with all of my heart. I pray that you will experience in ever-increasing ways the passions of our Lord.

Lastly, my loving wife, Micki. For 31 years you have been my best friend and faithful companion as together we sought and continue to seek to rekindle in our lives the flame of passion for our loving Lord.

Endorsements

Don, your book is on fire! To be left unchanged you'd have to read it with asbestos gloves and an iceberg heart. I read this book and went up in flames. This is fresh fire, fueled by the passion and pen of Don Milam. In fact, this book is so good I wished I had written it myself. It makes me want to quit preaching to focus, with fresh zeal, on rediscovering the lost passions of Jesus.

Tommy Tenney
Author of *The God Chasers* and *God's Favorite House*

Passion is more than strong emotion. It is expressed in our anger, sexuality, enthusiasm, and a love for others. *The Lost Passions of Jesus* could be just what you're looking for, to reignite your own passion for Jesus, for a new depth of spirituality and, therefore…your destiny.

Gerald Coates
Speaker, author, broadcaster

One of the worst places to be is in a hard-working church that has lost its passion for Jesus. The church in Ephesus received a letter from God saying that if they failed to respond to the dilemma, He would remove their lampstand.

Lack of passion reduces our ability to see God at work. Worldly blindness leads to hell. Christian blindness leads us into ignorance of God and

His ways. Passion is the restoration of first love that freshens our ability to remain current with God. We are all Pharisees being healed, and passion is the antidote. Don's book stirs my heart to love Jesus more. Take the time to read it slowly, contemplating its message. Take the inward journey to rediscover the passion that God has for you. Fail in this, and you fail in everything.

Graham Cooke
Author of *Developing Your Prophetic Gifting*
and *A Divine Confrontation*

Contents

Foreword

Our culture has lost its passion.

No, it is worse than that.

Our culture rejects passion.

It chooses, rather, cold, intellectual responses to life's most incredible opportunities. It has redefined what it means to love, to give, and to hold in high regard. Those natural impulses that make man who he is and that define his relationship to everything from God to Sunday afternoon football to how he sees his own family, are now analyzed and interpreted until all gentleness and inner personal resolve have little to do with success and personal fulfillment.

It seems that the most intelligent among us are those who have voluntarily replaced passion with analysis and emotion with reason.

The most compelling issues of life are now defined and scrutinized while inner feelings and personal desire are relegated to the apparently uninformed and the weak-minded. We have willingly surrendered the essence of our humanity, that ethereal sense of determination and will to succeed, to those who we have been told know better than the rest of us. These are the practitioners of calculated thought processes that judge everything according to a universal code of correctness that comes straight from the mind, totally bypassing the heart with all its desires and eternal passions.

Of course, many will come humphing to the defense of these mature societal changes, calling them reasonable responses to a more archaic time when a person pursued a life goal simply because he felt it deep inside his soul.

Such feelings are now replaced with tired, hollow opinions and objections that have kept our society and, more importantly, the Church, passive and ineffective at a time when we can afford neither.

Passion is the heart of who we are. Humanity cannot survive without passion anymore than a wheel can turn without grease or a kite can fly without wind or a song can be sung without air to carry its melody. Nonetheless, it is the passionate who always bear the accusation of being unstable, rebellious, and untrustworthy. Passion is no longer understood as an essential ingredient of the success of a man, a church, or a nation.

The religious system has contributed significantly to the demise of passion. It fears the passionate, understanding that the passionate always challenge the existing order of things. They always demand proof for why things are the way they are. They seldom accept tradition as the excuse for religion's troubling ways of mediocrity and intellectual ascent.

The passionate will continuously resist attempts to be controlled and silenced. Even in the midst of spurious accusations, the impassioned remain ablaze in their hearts. No wonder passionate people are feared by the system of religion that exists only to ensure its continuation throughout the generations. Call them rebellious, but they are merely passionate. They cannot acquiesce to the mundane or the predictable.

The aimless drift of passionless Christianity can never be masked by the continuous, faddish activities of those who purport to be her leaders. From the cold and darkened sanctuaries of our most traditional denominations to the swanky glitz of contemporary religion, that which once made our faith the life-giving, death-defying powerhouse of love it once was is all but gone.

Wooed by the opportunities of her wealth, covetous over the favor of her elite, the once discerning Church of our Lord has been drawn into the trap of world-pleasing, mind-tickling theology that has no love, no purpose, no impact, and no real reason to exist.

But there are troublemakers out there. These are men like Don Milam who see through the dazzle and are far from impressed. They are bored with lifeless tradition, inspite of the polished programs in which it is presented. These folks won't stop until they are fully empowered by the same passions that our Lord Jesus displayed when He walked the earth. They know that the world will only change when our Lord Jesus is once again building His glorious Church and He Himself plants inside of us the same fiery passions that ignited the early disciples.

The passions of our Lord cannot be acquired through programs, preaching or prophesying. They only come through our Lord Jesus Himself. Finally there are men and women who are tired of the outward showmanship that has cheapened our precious faith. They are looking for Him and Him alone.

Jesus Himself must build His own Church free from the man-made antics of a Christless Church system that fears Him and the passions He represents.

So, may our prayer be, "Come, Lord Jesus! Come in our hearts and bring all Your passion and all Your love. Open me to display the fullness of who You really are! Show Yourself through me with prayer, faith, and true Lordship deep in my heart. Give me courage to allow Your glory to shine through me. Help me to do what You are doing, to allow the Holy Spirit to work through me and help me take Your Presence to those who need You the most. Set my heart with only one desire: to display Your passions to the world. Amen."

Don Nori
Author of *No More Sour Grapes*
The Power of Brokenness, The Angel and the Judgment
His Manifest Presence, Secrets of the Most Holy Place
and *How to Find God's Love*

Introduction

IT IS MY PERSONAL STRONG CONVICTION that we in the Body of Christ are living in the midst of a major battle in these last days. The spirit of this world is continually raging against the Church of Jesus Christ to wear down the saints. It is a clash of passions that we are involved in! The Book of Revelation vividly paints for us the consequences and conditions of the Laodicean church age. Lukewarmness is the warning declared and passion for the Son of God is the remedy prescribed.

Consider the word for a moment...*passion*. What comes to your mind? Surely images of romance and intimacy are some of the first thoughts that circulate. The word *passion* can mean, "the emotions as distinguished from reason; intense, driving, or overmastering feeling; ardent affection; a strong liking for or devotion to some activity, object, or concept." But it is interesting to note that Webster's Dictionary, when defining the term *passion*, first describes it in the following manner: "the sufferings of Christ between the night of the Last Supper and his death; an oratorio based on a gospel narrative of the Passion." Isn't that amazing?! Passion relates to our relationship with God and to His relationship with us!

Yes, we are in a battle for the restoration of our first love for our great and glorious Messiah—Jesus Christ the Lord! We must call forth passionate Christianity across the earth once again. After all, is He worth anything less?

But ponder with me yet for another moment. Have you ever wondered what causes the heart of our Lord to beat a little faster, what makes the flicker of love to burn brighter in His heart? Truly, if we could put our ear to His heart, we could perhaps hear the pulsating rhythm of this echo beat ever louder as we mention the poor, the lost, our Father, and things called faith, hope, and love. Oh, to hear the heart of God! Indeed, embracing the passions of the Son of God is the medicine that the Church of this age needs!

That is what this book composed by my friend Don Milam is all about. It is about restoring to the Body of Christ the passions that are in His heart. As you read this book, you will go on a Church history journey with Don— a path less traveled in our hectic-paced society. Like a spiritual archaeologist, this book, *The Lost Passions of Jesus*, uncovers for us some of these treasures of the past.

Jewels from what some have referred to as the "Christian mystics"— such as Madame Guyon, Jacob Boehme, John Flavel and Sadhu Sundar Singh—are marvelously dusted off for us to look at. We also gaze at diamonds from some of the classical writers, such as Henry Drummond and Charles Price. Oh, what a treasure chest is opened up for us through this book!

Don understands the necessity of fanning into a flame *The Lost Passions of Jesus*. In recent years, Don himself found that his own heart and life needed reawakened with a passionate fire for the Son of God. Has that ever happened to you? Have you yourself ever needed heart surgery? If so, then I have good news for you. The contents of this book are loaded with devices that have been proven throughout the ages to charge a heart back into flaming love.

If you want to be charged up, then this book was written with you in mind. If you are looking for lasting remedies and not just modern quick fixes, then the prescription the doctor ordered is written throughout the pages of this fresh approach to *The Lost Passions of Jesus*. May you read and weep as I did.

Blessings to each of you!

Jim W. Goll
Author of *The Lost Art of Intercession*
and *Father, Forgive Us!*

Chapter 1

The Search for the Passions

WHAT INNER FORCE LIFTS A MAN out of the mainstream of
mediocrity and into the lonely chase of his dream? What mysterious power is so mesmerizing that it leads one to relinquish the luxuries of
life in order to respond to the lure of the unthinkable? What intriguing pursuit has the power to pull one into a circle of commitment that eliminates
all other fascinations outside that ring? What sacred cause awakens a man
from the slumber of indifference to pursue the scent of the impossible?

This strange phenomenon is called *passion*. Passion is the fire of life
and the energy of the soul! It is the wind that gives loft to the eagle, lifting
it above the masses locked in the drudgery of apathetic inactivity. It is the
fire that warms the heart in the midst of the coldness of a culture set adrift.
It is a man's friend in the dark hours of the night when others abandon him.
It is the inner support that keeps him awake in the night seasons when others are fast asleep. It is the power for the race, the propulsion for the jet, the
spark for the fire, the wind for the sail, and the contractions for the birth.

Every successful man and woman has experienced the transforming
power of passion. Like a silent hunter, this unseen force captured them with
its reality and catapulted them into the race for the inaccessible. These men
and women became its prisoners, coerced by the allurement of its dreams.

This kind of success demands that a man reach deep down within himself for an inner strength that can be produced only by this passionate zeal.

Passion brings forth a harvest of dreamers and visionaries. It is the dynamic link that connects a dream to its reality. A dream is not enough; it always must be accompanied by the intensity of passion that drives one into the lonely arena reserved for those who attempt the impossible and track the invisible.

Those who have not seen the invisible realities of their dream worlds think such people are mad. The contented are disturbed by their zeal and fervor. The elite misinterpret the driven actions of such people as a direct assault on them. All isolate them for fear of catching this horrible disease that challenges one to move outside the comfort of the traditional and conventional. They endeavor to segregate these people in order to safeguard their own comfortable and secure lifestyles.

Not every passion is legitimate. Some passions are destructive and even dangerous. The drive for wealth, fame, and power can motivate people to betrayal and domination of others. It can possess them to the point where they manipulate those around them and destroy their own souls.

In spite of the fact that some passions can be negative, you must understand that you cannot achieve anything without passion. Without the fire of passion a person will slip back into the slough of mediocrity and be tempted to return to the shelter of anonymity. The absence of passion will leave one isolated in his own fantasy world, always dreaming of the great possibilities of life but never committing himself to their fulfillment.

If you discover the passion behind a man's success, you will have found the key that unlocks the door to his dream world. When you find his dream, you will discover his heart. And when you find his heart, you will understand his actions. Few people in life are willing to expend the effort to understand those individuals in their midst who are attracted by the images of the inconceivable. They are too fearful that they might be infected by that fiery virus of passion and so be ruined.

With that in mind, let us ask ourselves this question: What was the compelling passion in the life of the Lord Jesus? Why did Jesus thrust Himself onto the road that led Him to His ultimate sacrifice? What was the fountainhead of that sacred devotion that continually put Him in contention with the ruling powers of His day? What dynamic energy pushed Him into the pool of the poor, placed Him in conflict with the fanaticism of the fundamentalist, piloted Him into the darkness of the desert, and eventually pinned Him to the cruelty of the cross? Then, when we are confronted with the powerful passion of this Man, what shall we offer as our illustration of passionate service?

Discovering the passions of Jesus is not a difficult task, but it does require that you lay down the intrigue of doctrinal issues, forfeit your crude theological concepts, and sacrifice your supporting proof texts that justify your own secure lifestyle.

This is not a theological investigation guided by the support of lexicons and commentaries. We are not going on a biblical hunt for more knowledge. Our minds are already overloaded with truth that has never reached our hearts. Rather, we are in pursuit of something that will change our hearts and ignite a fire in our souls.

If you search the Gospels for the veritable realities spoken from the mouth of Jesus and the zealous actions demonstrated by the hand of our Lord, you will find the key to His passions. From His lips He exposes the dreams that fuel His fervor. By His actions He exhibits the heart that activates His every move.

Each Gospel writer emphasized the intricate and multifaceted passions of our Lord. Two of the writers had not walked with Jesus during His earthly ministry (Mark and Luke), and the other two men had been at His side day after day (Matthew and John).

For Mark and Luke, the truths of which they wrote had already been communicated to the diverse Body of Christ in the first century. Someone had taken the time to follow the passion trail and discover the dream and vision of the Man. Maybe it was Mark and Luke who scouted out those truths as they interviewed one disciple after another. Perhaps, like detectives on the case, they followed each clue to its reasonable spiritual conclusion.

For Matthew and John it was much different. They had stood alongside Him. They had looked into His eyes. They had felt the warm, sweet breeze of His passion sweep over them. They had experienced the strength of His zeal invading their souls. They had been drawn into that inner circle where passion beats its strongest. The fire of passion had captured their hearts, and they had been ruined.

What were those passions, you ask? There are three guideposts in the Scriptures that help us to distinguish the passions of the Lord.

To identify the passions of the Son of God, first go to the man who was considered to be the closest to Him in that triumvirate circle of friends:

John. A man's closest friend can unveil something of the inner drive that propels him forward. An intimate friend is the one who is most in tune with his heart. Read John's writings and you will discover what things consumed this disciple concerning the passion of Jesus. It is not hard. They will leap out at you.

At the very beginning of Jesus' ministry, John was so affected by His fervor that he was reminded of the prophetic words of King David: "Zeal for Your house will consume me."[1]

John's account stands alone from the other three Gospels. His is not a historical treatise on the life of our Lord. John takes a totally different tack as he presents his testimony. The Gospel of John looks closer at the heart of the Lord Jesus. It is through John's words that we get the most intimate look at the passion of our Lord. John's words will help us greatly in our search.

Second, look at the words that Jesus uses at the beginning of His ministry. They serve as compelling evidence and will help you unravel the mystery of His motivations. For you see, Jesus' first public words will not be frivolous and unrehearsed. He has waited in eternity for this moment in time, and as He makes His way to the public stage of life, He will speak words that came with Him from the presence of His Father. He has many spiritual truths that He can introduce, but He is determined to avoid the rhetoric of the religious and instead attract them with the reality of Heaven's realm. The Sermon on the Mount will help us immensely with this part of our search.

Third and finally, you will want to turn to the end of each of the Gospels and look at the words of the Master at the conclusion of His life. When a man faces death, he inevitably focuses on the matters that consume his heart. He tries to deal with all unfinished business. Jesus is no different. He wants to leave with His friends those things that will prepare them for His absence. He eagerly details for them the critical issues that they must pass on to succeeding generations. Looking over the whole of His life, He condenses it into the most consequential truths that will prepare them for the tasks that lie before them.

The words and prayers of our Lord in the Upper Room are His last before He faces the injustices of His upcoming trial and the atrocity of the

---

1.   John 2:17.

cross. Here Jesus does not deal with the trivial or the unimportant. He reaches deep down into His soul and delivers the timeless passions of His life. He reviews His life and pulls out those words that must not be forgotten. These are the things that must be passed on. They must be remembered. In fact, He sends the Holy Spirit to remind His followers of these very truths.

John chapters 13–17, more than any other passage in the Bible, capsulizes the passion of our Lord in a most succinct and convincing way. They contain His last words to His disciples in a very intimate and personal setting. In these chapters we are invited to participate in the privacy surrounding that table in the Upper Room. Let your heart be arrested by those words as the Lord pours out His heart and spirit to His disciples and to His heavenly Father. There we find the private passions of Jesus. There we are most powerfully introduced to the fire of His life.

As John sat close to the side of his Master, he could feel the flame of passion burn in the Son's heart as Jesus contemplates His own death, the destiny of His disciples, and the future of the Church. Those things that He longs to see coming into reality resonate in His instructions to the disciples and His petitions to the Father.

These passions of the Lord flare up with great intensity in the early Church, but by the end of the first century they had already begun to diminish. The sword of persecution and the tests of heresies diminished the flame and reduced their capacity to contain the passion. Ritualism soon completed the destruction, and Jesus' passion disappeared almost completely from the Church.

In the succeeding chapters we will explore together the depth of Jesus' passions.

This is a journey.

It is a search for a new source of fuel to ignite us in this generation. Combined with our search for the passions of Jesus, we will look at some writings of various people of the past who maintained the fire of the Lord's heart. These are the words of those who also caught this passionate flame and were ruined!

Let it be our prayer that in these days our hearts be gripped with the passions that controlled and motivated the life of our Lord.

May you also be ruined by these passions of our Lord!

Chapter 2

Part I

The Passion for the Rule of God

SOME OF THE FIRST WORDS that we hear from the lips of the Son are, "Repent, for the *kingdom* of heaven is near."[1]

Matthew announced that Jesus initiated His public ministry by traveling throughout Galilee preaching the good news of the Kingdom.[2] This itinerant preaching throughout this tiny, backward land set up the beginning of Jesus' physical ministry on the earth. The Sermon on the Mount became His first recorded words as the new prophet on the scene. This historic word is His "State of the Union" address, and in it He sets forth the Divine principles that will govern the Kingdom He has come to proclaim. It is the constitution and bylaws of the heavenly rule. With these words He sets aside the existing religious order and establishes a new order that will be loyal and subject to the heavenly King. He brought from Heaven a brand-new form of government that does not depend upon political suppression, philosophical manipulation, or religious domination. The laws of this Kingdom are not

---

1.   Matthew 4:17.
2.   See Matthew 4:23.

contained in human words developed by rationalistic thought, but are a heavenly script written on the hearts of men.

The heavenly Kingdom collides with the religious systems.

Six times in Matthew chapter 5 He says, "You have heard that it was said...," and then goes on to say, "But I tell you...." In these six instances He places in dynamic contrast the petty traditions of external absurdities with His holy emphasis on the interior issues of the heart.

The Pharisees had taken the simple law of Moses and constructed a monstrous, convoluted system of "613 rules—248 commands and 365 prohibitions—and bolstered these rules with 1521 emendations."[3] On that momentous day, Jesus did not open the gate that would lead to pastures of easy moral living.

Instead, He pushes the envelope farther than any Pharisee could ever imagine. He brushes aside their crude forms of morality and dismisses their outward servitude to impossible religious restrictions. He forever fixes morality in the arena of the concealed corners of the heart. In that first sermon, He establishes non-violence as the basis for how to deal with the aggressions in men's hearts. He newly defines adultery as no longer a forbidden sin of the flesh, but a thought and intent of the heart. Righteousness, He declares, to their consternation and amazement, is not a scrupulous observing of rules and regulations regarding actions. Rather, it is a heavenly Kingdom standard that puts the emphasis on man's internal thoughts and desires. The Kingdom is outwardly expressed in loving God and loving your brother as yourself.

It is almost impossible for us to imagine what it must have been like to sit on that crowded hillside listening to those amazing, almost blasphemous words for the very first time. We are centuries removed from the sound of those words, and the mists of time have diluted their spiritual impact. The acrid theological smog and the permissive thinking of our day have clouded our imaginative power to comprehend the storm of controversy that Jesus' words aroused. Much pulpit preaching and our own repetitive reading of this account have diminished the transcendent power of those words upon our spirits. We have read them over and over. We have memorized them and contemplated their meaning. We have heard them preached and

---

3.   Philip Yancey, *The Jesus I Never Knew* (Grand Rapids, Michigan: Zondervan Publishing House, 1995), 132.

dissected so many times that they have been rendered almost void of their deepest spiritual import.

But those who sat listening on that hillside so long ago were hearing words never before uttered by their rabbis or any other in their recorded history. In a state of shock—almost disbelief—they listened to these life-giving declarations that issued forth from an itinerant preacher who spoke as no man had ever spoken before in their remembrance. He spoke as one familiar with the God they could only hope to appease by their ritualistic observance of the myriad laws passed down from their fathers. The God this Man spoke of did not appear to be harsh and demanding, but truly yearning for their friendship. Like an ambassador of an otherworldly kingdom, He spoke with authority about the Kingdom of Heaven. He assured them that the spoils of the Kingdom were greater than the pain, poverty, or persecution they might be called upon to endure.

His speech was very different from the religious teachers of that day, but the attraction was more than the words that He spoke. The common people could actually feel His love and deep yearning for their spiritual and physical wholeness emanating from His very being. They sat in blessed bewilderment as waves of mercy swept over them. They gathered as close as they could get to this Teacher. Never had they sensed such compassion and caring from the holy men of their day.

They were more accustomed to rigid instruction delivered with harshness. They were more familiar with declarations that Yahweh, the God of Abraham, Isaac, and Jacob, could be pleased with the likes of them only by their unquestioning, legalistic adherence to ceremonial rules and regulations. Their only true hope lay in a future idyllic world where they would play some small part in an earthly kingdom ushered in by a conquering Messiah.

What they heard from their religious leaders, year after year, were words that weighed them down with impossible requirements and that were devoid of any hope as to how to meet them. Taking the spiritual words of Moses and the prophets, the Pharisees added their own, seemingly endless detailed definitions and twisted interpretations. Their desire was a religion designed to serve their own political agendas. They created a system that touted them as the qualified, "chosen learned ones" who alone could explain the holy writings and the mysteries of God to the common man.

They anticipated a future political kingdom in which they would, naturally, be the rulers and dispensers of the edicts from the Throne.

Then along comes this carpenter, with His pronouncements of love and acceptance, who threatens their previously unquestioned position and power in the nation.[4] But the Kingdom that Jesus spoke of was not a kingdom of earthly power and suppression. It did not require its citizens to work their way up a ladder of worthiness by fearful adherence to obscure and impossible rules and regulations, enforced with legalism and religious manipulation. They, the respected, prestigious hierarchy of Israel, knew that they would never be at the center of that otherworldly kingdom, and that they could not accept. He must die!

The Kingdom of God has come near!

Now having been questioned by the Pharisees as to when the kingdom of God was coming, He answered them and said, "The kingdom of God is not coming with signs to be observed; nor will they say, 'Look, here it is!' or, 'There it is!' For behold, the kingdom of God is in your midst" (Luke 17:20-21).

All of Israel was consumed with this issue of the Kingdom. However, they were looking for an apocalyptic kingdom that would usher in all that they had dreamed of. Their misguided illusions of grandeur caused them to miss the very dynamic of God right in their midst. They were looking for something tangible and powerful. They were expecting a ruler, a Messiah, who would establish them again in Solomon-like splendor, far above the other nations of the world.

All that the Kingdom encompassed is standing right before their very eyes, and they miss it. Their spiritual paradigms cause them to miss their appointment with God!

To encounter Jesus was to encounter the Kingdom! The very Kingdom that they were anxiously awaiting stood right in their midst, but they did not perceive it. Rather, the Kingdom that Jesus came to establish would begin in the hearts of men. It would not come by military subjugation or religious manipulation, but by a spiritual transformation. As His rule would grow stronger in the hearts of His disciples, they would recognize that the Kingdom was among them and that the Door was their beloved Master.

---

4.   See John 11:48.

The Kingdom of God is come when the will of God is done.

Jesus said, "Thy kingdom come. Thy will be done, on earth as it is in heaven."[5]

On another occasion He proclaimed, "Not everyone who says to Me, 'Lord, Lord,' will enter the kingdom of heaven; but he who does the will of My Father who is in heaven."[6]

Submission to the will of the Father is the single most important Kingdom precept. Choosing to yield our stubborn, self-absorbed human will to a higher will—the will we rejected in the Garden of Eden—is the doorway through which the Kingdom comes and dwells among men. The world witnesses, even if it does not understand, that another "government" is present when it sees ordinary men and women voluntarily choosing to lay aside their own plans and choices to walk in joyful obedience to their God.

It was this passion for His Father's will that drove the Lord Jesus. Listen to His words:

... "*Truly, truly, I say to you, the Son can do nothing of Himself, unless it is something He sees the Father doing; for whatever the Father does, these things the Son also does in like manner*" (John 5:19).

... "*When you lift up the Son of Man, then you will know that I am He, and I do nothing on My own initiative, but I speak these things as the Father taught Me*" (John 8:28).

I can do nothing on My own initiative. As I hear, I judge; and My judgment is just, because I do not seek My own will, but the will of Him who sent Me (John 5:30).

The mysteries of the Kingdom are locked away in the hidden place.

The secret to the Kingdom is not to be found in mere legalistic conformity to rules or in the practice of self-denial and asceticism. It will not be unlocked in the maze of religious rhetoric that is often preached from the pulpits of our day. It is not to be found in denominational hierarchy or religious movements. It will not be uncovered in private ministries that seek public exposure. It will *only* be found in the hidden places!

---

5.   Matthew 6:10.
6.   Matthew 7:21.

He spoke another parable to them, "The kingdom of heaven is like leaven, which a woman took, and hid in three pecks of meal, until it was all leavened" (Matthew 13:33).

The kingdom of heaven is like a treasure hidden in the field, which a man found and hid; and from joy over it he goes and sells all that he has, and buys that field (Matthew 13:44).

The Kingdom of Heaven will be found hidden in the deep recesses of the hearts of those men and women who hear the still, small voice of the Father and who with their whole being respond, "Yes, my Lord."

One mystery of the Kingdom of which Jesus spoke is its hiddenness. In parabolic form Jesus spoke of the Kingdom as a seed planted in a field, a treasure hidden in the field, leaven dispersed in the dough, and a pearl hidden away. Why should something so powerful be kept hidden? It is because we do not know what we are looking for! If you have been deluded into believing that the Kingdom is a powerful, commonly accepted nationalistic institution led by highly efficient and greatly talented men, then you are doomed to miss it.

God has chosen for this Kingdom to start as a small seed, planted and hidden away. The Kingdom seed is hidden in the hearts of men and women. It takes time and faith for it to germinate and to grow and mature. Similarly, God tucks the man or woman of His choosing away in a solitary place so that the germination and maturing process can proceed without interference.

Tragically, many are lost during that process. Too impatient to let the seed form and mature, they launch out on their own—and so pull the seed out of the ground before its time. Refusing to submit to the Divine Will, they die to their Kingdom destiny. Denominational institutions, all too glad to receive them into their hallowed halls of learning, train them in the ways of religion and then send them out to die. They die as a result of their own ambitions, pride, and lack of real spiritual preparation. *They were taught the Word, but they did not allow the Word to teach them!*

In God's great mercy, though, a Seed has been planted in the hearts of many, and the time for maturation is inevitable. When it bursts forth in life, the Kingdom is manifested, obscured no longer to the nations and peoples of the earth. At that time, the Divine Life will have developed into maturity within the lives of the messengers and will burst its confines to impact every institution and government that exists around the world.

This seed will spread into society.
It will permeate the cultures.
It will bring down religious orders.
It will disturb the comfortable.
It will awaken sleeping giants.
It will confront the tragedies of life.
It will bring hope to the hopeless.
It will address the afflictions of society.
It will move in earth-shaking power.
It is the Word of Life!

Entrance into the Kingdom of God is a child thing!

... *"I tell you the truth, unless you change and become like little children, you will never enter the kingdom of heaven. Therefore, whoever humbles himself like this child is the greatest in the kingdom of heaven"* (Matthew 18:3-4 NIV).

But Jesus said, "Let the children alone, and do not hinder them from coming to Me; for the kingdom of heaven belongs to such as these" (Matthew 19:14).

But when Jesus saw this, He was indignant and said to them, "Permit the children to come to Me; do not hinder them; for the kingdom of God belongs to such as these. Truly I say to you, whoever does not receive the kingdom of God like a child shall not enter it at all" (Mark 10:14-15).

To enter the Kingdom of Heaven, a man must bow down low and, figuratively speaking, crawl through the gate of salvation. The Kingdom will never be possessed by the haughty and proud. It will always be illusive to those who promote themselves and magnify their works and ministries, grabbing their recognition before it is time. The laws of the Kingdom dictate that a man can enter in only with the spirit of a child, the brokenness of the humble, the attitude of the lowly, and the simplicity of the innocent. This Kingdom stands in stark contrast to the religion of our day that exalts the proud, honors the successful, idolizes the talented and gifted, and rejoices in the accolades of others.

This Kingdom is occupied only by the poor in spirit, the merciful, the pure in heart, the peacemakers, the persecuted, and those who hunger after righteousness. It is a Kingdom of another world. If we truly believe the beatitudes that Jesus spoke, then why do we demean spiritual poverty, mercy, purity, and persecution rather than embrace them as the blessed qualifications for the Kingdom that our Lord proposed? Jesus aligned Himself with the poor and disenfranchised while we prefer to be found among the materially fortunate and spiritually important. We leave the poor to their hopelessness and curry the favor of the rich in our society, for they are necessary to the ongoing support of our own kingdoms. *We enforce the subtle separation of God's people by our denominational, social, and racial mind-sets!*

Greatness in God's Kingdom is measured by humble obedience, servanthood, embracing the cross, recognizing our insufficiencies, and utter dependence on a Source greater than ourselves. Kingdom fame is found in some very unlikely places. It is not necessarily found on a platform before great audiences. It might be found in a prayer closet. It might be found in a man who is faithfully doing his daily, ordinary job. It might be found in the home where a mother lovingly cares for her children. It might be found in a Sunday school room where a teacher pours out her soul to young children. Or it might be found in such unlikely places as a rescue center, where one cares for the hurting and deprived. We might be surprised to find it in businesses where everyday men and women, as living epistles, are read by men in the marketplaces of the world. You never know where greatness might be found. But God's eye does not miss one deed done in His name.

The Kingdom of God is not of this world!

Again listen to the words of the Son: "My kingdom is not of this world. If it were, My servants would fight to prevent My arrest by the Jews. *But now My kingdom is from another place.*"[7]

The Kingdom of God exists in a parallel dimension that, through the Spirit of God, is inexorably invading the material realm of man, capturing the hearts and allegiance of men and women who are searching for their place in the Divine Plan.

You do not gain citizenship in that Kingdom by who you are, how much you have, or how educated you are. Only one thing qualifies a man or woman for that great privilege, and that is being born of water and the

—————————————
7.   John 18:36 NIV.

Spirit.[8] Washing in the redemptive blood of the Lamb that was slain before the foundation of the world is your holy preparation for entering that Spirit realm. Being birthed by the Spirit of God is the seal upon the citizen of this heavenly Kingdom. Living by the power of that Spirit every day, the citizen finds himself uniquely qualified to enforce the claims of the Kingdom upon his own life and upon the world around him.

Our natural birth delivers us into a physical realm where we are under the dictate and control of fixed natural laws that have terrible consequences if they are ignored. In order to experience the reality of Kingdom life, we must once more experience the pangs of birth—but this birth delivers us into a new spiritual realm, which has equally immutable laws.

Geoffrey Bull uses this wonderful illustration in his book, *The Sky Is Red*: "On a farm a duck may eat a worm, and a fox may eat a duck, then the farmer may shoot the fox, but none of these understands the nature of the creature above it."[9]

Life in the Spirit is not subject to life in the physical realm. It's a higher life. Those who live in the Kingdom realm of the Spirit are subject to laws that supersede the laws of nature. Jesus was never limited by or subject to the rules of the natural world. This "spirit Man" transcended those laws as He walked on the water, disappeared from a crowd that was ready to kill Him, and rose into the clouds as He departed this earth.

The realm of the natural places priority on reputation, advantage, position, control, wealth, self-reliance, revenge, and power. By contrast, the rules of the Kingdom of Heaven seem paradoxical and illogical. This realm places priority on qualities such as transparency, servanthood, humility, submission, mercy, hiddenness, self-control, and forgiveness. In the Kingdom realm, the way up is the way down. By Kingdom laws, the way to save one's life is to lose it. Only through a life-changing experience with the Eternal God who is Spirit, can man ever hope to be a citizen in such a Kingdom.

Jesus came from the invisible spirit world where His Father dwells with a power and authority to engage the forces of this fallen world and enforce the laws of the Kingdom of Heaven upon every demonic stronghold.

---

8. See John 3:5.
9. Geoffrey Bull, *The Sky Is Red* (Hodder & Stoughton Ltd., 1965; London: Pickering & Inglis, 1981), 136.

Culturally relevant, this Kingdom holds within it the answers to the perplexities and troubles of this world. It has within it the power to change the very fabric of society. But that power can be activated only when the fibers of men's hearts are gathered into the Master's hands and woven into a new tapestry of self-denial. If hearts are not changed, all our church-imposed do's and don'ts will do no good. *The Kingdom way is a higher way!*

The Kingdom is inaugurated by a death!

While most men are driven by the never-ending pursuit of life and immortality, Jesus was driven by the pursuit of Calvary and its horrible death. His face was always set toward Jerusalem. To inaugurate the Kingdom that He spent three years preaching about to the disenfranchised, Jesus suffered untold indignities at the hands of His creation and died a lonely, torturous death. There on the cross He endured the greatest pain He had ever known: separation from His beloved Father. This eternal, immortal Seed, the Second Adam, was buried in the earth of humanity and then arose and burst through the confines of time and space to plant the flag of a new Kingdom on the earth—the Kingdom of God!

This rule of God would be so otherworldly that it would require those desiring to enter into its domain to die in order to live by its precepts. They must experience death in order to truly experience life. Death to self is the only appropriate seedbed in which to plant this new seed of the Spirit. Then, as the fresh rains of Heaven water it and the eternal Bread of Life feeds it, that seed begins to take on its own spiritual form.

The Kingdom comes in direct conflict with satanic influences!

And Jesus was going about in all Galilee, teaching in their synagogues, and proclaiming the gospel of the kingdom, and healing every kind of disease and every kind of sickness among the people (Matthew 4:23).

But if I cast out demons by the Spirit of God, then the kingdom of God has come upon you (Matthew 12:28).

It is totally impossible for two diametrically opposed kingdoms to exist together; one will overwhelm the other. Religion, though, has learned to coexist with the evil around it. In fact, religion has always found a way to cohabit with evil.

But it was not so with this Man or the rule that He had come to establish! He could not ignore the suffering and suppression that the enemy had imposed upon the people. Everywhere the message of the Kingdom was proclaimed, the power of that Kingdom was demonstrated. Wherever He found the smallest measure of faith, disease was rebuked, demons expelled, sin forgiven, and people freed.

That is the great contrast between the spiritual Kingdom He had come to establish and the religious order that men establish. Religion can permit sin to exist and can easily ignore the oppression and pain of its constituents. Religion does not find it difficult to compromise with the forces of the dark side.

Wherever the Kingdom of God is manifest, however, there is no compromise. Sin must be removed, healing must come, oppression must stop, evil must be destroyed, and compassion must reign.

Down through the centuries the political posturing of religious men obscured our Lord's passion for the Kingdom. The Kingdom message was twisted and reworked until it accommodated the vagrancies of the religious system that it was to replace. The Kingdom message emphasized the heart and the need for change, but as theologians shifted it away from the interior issues of the heart, it developed into a matrix of eschatology.

Nevertheless, through the centuries there have been those who guarded the true essence of the Lord's passion for the rule of God being established in man. Jacob Boehme was one of those men. He had a clear understanding of the conflict that exists between the kingdom of the soul and the Kingdom of God. He accurately and effectively described the process of the Kingdom's taking its reign in the soul of man. Jacob Boehme is a man who wrestled with these truths and reflected the passion of our Lord for the birth of the Kingdom in man.

Chapter 2

Part II

The Image of the Heavenly[1]

Jacob Boeme

...John Westley, in his day, required all of his preachers to study the writings of Jacob Boehme; and the learned English theologian, William Law, said of him: "Jacob Boehme was not a messenger of anything new in religion, but the mystery of all that was old and true in religion and nature, was opened up to him,—the depth of the riches, both of the wisdom and knowledge of God."

Born of poor, but pious, Lutheran parents, from childhood Jacob Boehme was concerned about "the salvation of his soul." Although occupied, first as a Shepherd, and afterward as a shoemaker, he was always an earnest student of the Holy Scriptures; but he could not understand "the ways of God," and he became "perplexed, even to melancholy,—pressed out of measure." He said, "I knew the Bible from beginning to end but I could find no consolation in Holy Writ; and my spirit, as if moving in a great storm, arose in God, carrying with it my whole heart, mind and will, and wrestled with the love and mercy of God, that his blessing might descend upon me, that my mind might be illumined with his Holy Spirit, that I might understand His will and get rid of my sorrow...."

---

1. Gary Sigler, "Jacob Boeme: The Image of the Heavenly." August 28, 1998. September 16, 1999. <http://www.sigler.org/boeme/>. Article reprinted by permission. Reprinted as is.

"I had always thought much of how I might inherit the *kingdom* [emphasis added] of heaven; but finding in myself a powerful opposition, in the desires that belong in the flesh and blood, I began a battle against my corrupted nature; and with the aid of God, made up my mind to overcome the inherited evil will,....break it, and enter wholly into the love of God in Christ Jesus. I sought the heart of Jesus Christ, the center of all truth; and I resolved to regard myself as dead in my inherited form, until the Spirit of God would take form in me, so that in and through Him, I might conduct my life.

"I stood in this resolution, fighting a battle with myself, until the light of the Spirit, a light entirely foreign to my unruly nature, began to break through the clouds. Then, after some farther hard fights with the powers of darkness, my spirit broke through the door of hell, and penetrated even unto the innermost essence of its newly born divinity where it was received with great love, as a bridegroom welcomes his beloved bride.

"No words can express the great joy and triumph I experienced, as of a life out of death, as of a resurrection from the dead! While in this state, as I was walking through a field of flowers, in fifteen minutes, I saw the mystery of creation, the original of this world and of all creatures... Then for seven days I was in a continual state of ecstasy, surrounded by the light of the Spirit, which immersed me in contemplation and happiness. I learned what God is and what is His will... I knew not how this happened to me, but my heart admired and praised the Lord for it!"

...From 1612 to 1624, he wrote thirty books. "My books are written," Boeme said, "only for those who desire to be sanctified and united to God, from whom they came. Not through my understanding, but in my resignation in Christ, from him, have I received knowledge of his mysteries. God dwells in that which will resign itself up, with all its reason and skill, unto him. I have prayed strongly that I might not write except for the glory of God and the instruction and benefit of my brothers."

Jacob Boehme's persecutions and sufferings began with the publication of his first book at the age of thirty five. Then, notwithstanding five years of enforced silence, banishment from his home town, and an ecclesiastical trial for heresy, his "interior wisdom" began to be recognized by the nobility of Germany; but at this time, at the age of forty nine, Boehme died, "happy," as he said, "in the midst of the heavenly music of the paradise of God."

MAN IN "THE IMAGE OF THE HEAVENLY"

"O great and holy God, I pray thee, set open my inwardness to me; that I may rightly know what I am; and open in me what was shut up in Adam.

"God stirred himself to produce creation. He was desirous of having children of his own kind. Creation was an act of the free will of God; God unfolded his eternal nature, and through his active love, or desire, he caused that which heretofore had been in him merely as spirit (as an image contained in a piece of wood before the artist has cut it out), to become substantial, corporeal.

"God longed after the visible substance of his similitude and image, and so created man. Man was created the child of Omnipotence; a pure virgin, after the form of the Eternal,...with a pure mind and holy faculties, in which dwelt no lust. His will was in God. He was to be a perfect symbol of God; to attain the great fountain of meekness and love welling up from the heart of God. He was a virgin without a feminine form, after the form of the Eternal; full of chastity, modesty and purity, in the Image of God.

"He had both Fire and Light in him, and therefore, Love. No knowledge of any evil was in him; no lust, no covetousness, no pride, no envy, no anger, nothing but love. The celestial image clothed him with divine power. He could have removed mountains with a word; he could rule over the sun, moon and stars; all was in his power, the fire, the air, the water and the earth. Every living creature feared him. His life fluid was heavenly. His will was in God, and God was in him. He was in paradise, clothed with the heavenly glory, the light of the majesty of God. He lived on paradisiacal fruit and the Word of God. He knew no woe, no sickness, no death; he lived in joy and delight, without toil or care.

"Man was created free and responsible, with a will to move in whatever direction he chose; to be nothing in himself, to be one with God; and in freedom to pass into that of the Son, to give all and to receive all from the Father, for the glory and power of God; or — to enter and remain in the world of darkness. For he was the son of God, and could have gone on into the manifestation of God, and God's deeds of wonder!

"Understand, O man, what thou wast before the fall; created to live eternally in love! Know how sin arose, that thou mayst lay hold of the remedy of it!

"God created His image and likeness in a single man. Adam was a man and also a woman; for God did not, in the beginning make man and woman; He did not create them at the same time, because the life in which the two properties of masculine and feminine are united in one, constitutes man in the image of God, after the manner of the Father's and the Son's property, which together are one God, not divided; for perfect love is not found in one property, but in the two, one entering into the other.

"The fire and light (which is the meekness and love of God) was in Adam. The fire of God is the root of all things, and the origin of life, the cause of all strength and power. Lucifer took offense at the light, the humility of God, and entered into the fierce might of the fire, for he would domineer. He turned away from the will of the Eternal, for the fierce power of the fire delighted him more that the meekness in the still habitation of God, and he became the prince of this world. He ever moveth in a fire which consumeth all else to himself. The devil's fire desires a body to devour, and turn to nothing, to darkness.

"God's fire is coupled with love; his fire causes light; and light, love; light desireth substance, a body to fill and does not consume; it takes away nothing, but it quickens; love giveth itself freely to all. The natural comprehendeth not light. Light changeth the false imagination into the truth. Fire alone makes a hard set self-hood. God moveth in the light of meekness, and hath substance, water, 'the water of life,' which holds fire captive. 'The water of life' alone can make immortal bodies.

"Adam could have generated a heavenly *kingdom* [emphasis added] out of himself....Eve was within Adam as a pure, chaste, virginal power. He could then generate in a virginal state, and procreate by means of his will, and out of his substance, without pain or laceration; for one being could have been born from another, in the same way as Adam in his virginal state, was projected into being in the image of God; because that which is of the Eternal, can also procreate, multiply itself, according to the law of Eternity. In time there was to have been born the King of all men, who was to take possession of God's *kingdom* [emphasis added], as Ruler of all created Beings, in place of cast-out Lucifer, now prince of this world.

"Adam saw within himself two forms of being, belonging to the paradisiacal world; and then he saw one also without, belonging to this world; and his soul imagined after the outward. Then came the command to him, 'Eat not of the mixed fruit of good and evil, lest ye die!' But Adam continued to imagine after the earthly dominion; he imagined after the beasts and introduced himself into bestial lust, to eat and to generate as beasts do. He desired to live in himself and be Lord. He thought he would eat both the paradisiacal and the forbidden fruit and so live forever; but he had brought the earthly quality into the pure, celestial substance, and his light was being extinguished; the divine image was disappearing, the earthly appearing.

"He could no longer live in obedience to the will of the Father; his lust for the earthly fruit overcame him; and he sank into a deep sleep; and God saw that it was not possible for him to live in obedience, and let him sleep; sleep signifieth death.

"So Adam cast himself out from the majesty of God, with his own will; he could not continue to walk in his innocency, that he might have his confirmation in the divine way of production; for he had turned from 'the speaking of the Word' into self-will, lust and 'speaking good and evil;' and God's good will perished in him.

"God had forbidden Adam his false desire, lust after earthly fruit and power and virtue; and Adam had no necessity for these things; he had the paradisiacal fruit, the Word of God, and no want or death. His eyes, which might have continued to see always and eternally the glory of God, closed in sleep. God permitted Adam to sleep; otherwise, in the power of fire, in his selfishness, he would have become a devil."

MAN IN "THE IMAGE OF THE EARTHY"

"We Have Borne the Image of the Earthy"

"Adam was given that which he would have, the terrestrial woman, in place of the celestial virgin; for Adam's treachery toward his heavenly consort, disqualified him for her, and left him only fitted for an 'Eve.' During his sleep, the woman was made out of Adam, and the image of God was destroyed. The man and the woman were made into creatures of this outer world, fashioned into mortality.

"Adam and Eve had still a paradisiacal consciousness, but mixed with terrestrial desire. They were 'naked' although 'not ashamed' until they had eaten of the earthly fruit. Adam went out from the will of God into the world, and was captivated by it, and ate of earthly fruit. Then the spirit of this world took his soul captive, and his faculties became earthly his substance bestial.

"After eating of the tree of self-knowledge, of good and evil, by willing otherwise than God willed, man became unholy; he died to the holy, heavenly image, and lived in the awakened bestial image of the serpent. The animal being had swallowed up the celestial state, and Adam and Eve then had common flesh, hard bones, bestial members, and needed bestial clothing.

"Man was now separated from God: Lusting after the earthly, the holy anointing oil, given of Christ, was dried up; he became shut up in a gross, bestial image, for his flesh now belonged to the earth and to death; the dominion of this world now dwelt in him.

"The desire of a beast is only to nourish itself and to multiply itself. It hath no understanding of any higher thing. It hath its own spirit, whereby it liveth and groweth and consumeth itself. If God had intended that man should live as the beasts, he would have created him in the similitude of, and with the beasts. If he had created him for this earthly, miserable, naked, toilsome, corruptible, animal life, He would have made men and women from the start; and both sexes would have come forth in the 'spoken word,' into the division of both properites, as it was in other earthly creatures.

"Lust originated in Adam, but thereupon his perverted desire began to be excited in the woman. Eve was then moved by her lust, which the devil awakened in her, and desiring to be skillful, she became foolish. The serpent said to her, 'Your eyes shall be opened, and you shall be as gods.' It is true that her earthly eyes were opened, but her spiritual eyes became closed; with earthly eyes, man cannot see the *kingdom* [emphasis added] of God.

"When Adam took notice of his bestial form, he was ashamed, and God said; 'Adam, where art thou?' His body did hide itself, so ashamed was his poor soul and he said, 'I was afraid; I was naked, and hid myself.' The precious heavenly virgin, with which he was clothed, was lost; his crystalline image was destroyed.

"After the fall, man was subject to the limitations of time, and was degraded to the animal state of being, so that heaven, paradise and divinity became a mystery to him. God cursed the earth for man's sake, and no paradisiacal fruit grew anymore; all was gone, save only the mercy and the grace of God! After the fall, men lived in weakness, as today. They begat children in two *kingdoms* [emphasis added] of wrath and love, evil and good, Cain and Abel, Ishmael and Isaac, Esau and Jacob.

"When man fell, the paradise of all heavenly knowledge withdrew, and wisdom was in grief until God gave the promise of the seed of the woman."

MAN IN THE RESTORED IMAGE

"We Shall Also Bear the Image of the Heavenly"

"All the teachings of Christ have no other object than to show us how we may re-ascend to our virginal unity with him. There is ever a strife over man's image; the devil and hell say, 'It is mine, by right of nature; it is generated out of my root.' The spirit of this world says, 'It is mine, I give it life, nourishment, and bring it up, and give to it my power and wonders.' The *kingdom* [emphasis added] of God says, 'I have set my heart upon it; I have regenerated it; I sought and found it; it is mine. It is now in my *kingdom* [emphasis added], and it must reveal my wonders.' And the poor soul of man is in continual warfare.

"O man, when the devil seeks to hinder thee, set thyself against him; oppose him strongly! Thou hast, in Christ, far greater power than he! Take all thy sins and cast them at the devil. 'I take the mercy of God, the death of Christ, to myself! Therein will I roll myself' For the last Adam was the Offering and the Liberator to set thee free!

"Cease to please thyself, and keep from thy natural will, then wilt thou fall into the will of God; and then the devil cannot meddle with thee! Man's own will brought him to his own center, separated from God. Man began in the Word of God, but broke off from it; he must come back and be regenerated, to become as he was made originally, inbreathed by God.

"The heavenly image, lost in Adam, the light-life of Christ, has been the birth-right of man ever since the 'treader down' of the serpent of self-will was promised. Christ restores this image through regeneration, by which man re-enters into the One Tree, Christ. This divine fire of the Spirit of Christ continually crushes the head of the serpent, i.e. the desire of the flesh, beneath his feet. For the devil ever holdeth before the soul the unclean forbidden tree; for he would have inward dominion in man. When man yieldeth himself wholly to God, his will falls again into the unsearchable will of God.

"Such a man as Adam was before his Eve, shall arise again, and enter into, and eternally possess paradise...Man will enter again into the 'speaking Word' and speak with God!

"The image of God is the fair virgin, which substantiated by the regenerate life, restores to man the wife of his youth (Mal. 2:14), the divine womanhood of Adam's two-fold perfection. This image, shut up in Adam, could only be stirred by the power of God, that it might again appear, God manifested himself in Christ. The eternal virginity, lost by Adam, came unto Mary by the Word of Life. The fire of divine love in her being, in the virginal essence, (corrupted in Adam, and now restored), brought to birth that 'Holy Thing', the Son of God. And Christ in man makes man alive; restores again that which the devil severed in the first Adam (into the male and female), making them one again,—a virginal manhood,—a son of God.

"Christ, the divine spiritual Sun of Righteousness, enters again into the original matrix, out of which the life of man has taken its origin,—the eternal Word. The hungry soul absorbs the Word and then returns to the original spiritual state, and becomes a temple of divine love, wherein the Father receives his beloved Son; and in which the Holy Spirit dwells. The creature is not God, it remaineth eternally under God; but God blazeth through it with his love-fire, his light and shining; and that shining, man retaineth as long as his will remaineth in God's light. Where the will is, there is the heart also.

"As Christ was born in a stable, and cradled in a manger, so is Christ in man ever born amidst the animals in man. The newborn Savior is ever laid in a cradle between the ox of self-will and the ass of ignorance, in the stable of the animal condition in man; and from thence the king of pride (as Herod), finds his *kingdom* [emphasis added] endangered, and seeks to kill the child, who is to become the ruler of the 'New Jerusalem' in man.

"O man, take heed of pride; the devil fleeth into it! Take heed of covetousness! The covetous man is the greatest fool upon earth; he gathers that which he must leave to others, and gains only an evil conscience and treasures in hell! But as he that trusteth God hath continually enough; he gets a new body, which neither hunger, cold, nor heat, can affect; he hath a conscience at rest, and will eternally rejoice in his treasure he has laid up in heaven! Take heed of anger; that is the devil's sword, with which he commits all murders. If the soul is given to lust, pleasure and dominion of this world, the devil doth not sift it so strongly; he carrieth it in his triumphant chariot! Take heed of the perfect pattern God has given, of what man should, and must be,—Jesus! And pray for the illumination of the Holy Spirit; resolve not to let him go, until he bless thee!

"The Holy Spirit, the moving power of God, the former of his Word, which expresseth the will of God, the heart of God, openeth the heart of man to the virtues of God's Word. Then the animal within must die! One cannot remain an animal and become divine. When the soul is freed from the evil beast, then it is open to Christ, and His divine love-fire. God's Son is love and light and life; for man to pass from fire to light, there is only one way, through death.

"Man must cease to act by his false imagination; he must put it to death—into the hiddenness, nail it to the cross of Christ; and there, through lack of indulgence, nourishment, it dies; and then comes the 'new-birth',—light, liberty and love! By the power of the light and love of Christ, man overcomes the fire of self-will, and reestablishes his soul in the divine image of God. Then must he keep his imagination fixed in the love of God; for all outside is darkness.

"The two *kingdoms* [emphasis added] of fire and light, — wrath and love, part at the cross. On the cross the Son of God redeemed the soul unto the heavenly image, the Word, the eternal Body of Christ, which is heavenly. In Christ the divine *kingdom* [emphasis added] standeth open, and every one that will, may enter in; whosoever puts his will away from himself, and puts it into Christ, when that soul is born of the Word and the Spirit of Christ, then the inward body of the soul becometh a new creation in Christ; God and this inward man become one. Mortification of self-will and the recipiency of grace, is all a human can do to work out his own salvation.

"The going on 'to perfection,' includes both an increase of knowledge, and the greatest holiness of life. Sin must be brought into the judgment of God, and the holy love fire of God must consume it. When the will is converted, the soul enters into such sorrow for earthly iniquity that it will have nothing of iniquity any more.

"The regenerated, new-born soul in Christ has not only a new spirit, but is a new creation, with an everlasting (spiritual) body. He is not of this world; he is a stranger to this world, with no understanding of it. He is in the paradise of God, and desires nothing else but that which Christ within his soul desires. This soul must die to letters, reason, scholarship and knowledge, to enter into the only one true life—Jesus! For hard thoughts, high fancies and conceits are not necessary, but the love and mercy of God—to be one with Him. This soul must keep plunged in the humility, love and patience of God; go every hour out of death, and into life!

"He must learn how to go out of discussion and vanity; break the power of the selfish will, which no man can do by his own human power. He must give up his self-will as dead, that he may be submerged in the love of God. To every self-centered desire this soul must die; for all that doth vex and plague is the self-hood. In all the world there is no such cruel beast as that which is in the heart of every man and woman,—self-love!

"What hinders men from seeing and hearing God, is their own hearing, seeing and willing; by their own wills they separate themselves from the will of God. They see and hear within their own desires, which obstructs them from seeing and hearing God. Terrestrial and material things overshadow them, and they cannot see beyond their own human nature. If they would be still, desist from thinking and feeling with their own self-hood, subdue the self-will, enter into a state of resignation, into a divine union with Christ, who sees God, and hears God, and speaks with him, who knows the word and will of God; then would the eternal hearing, seeing and speaking become revealed to them. Self-will cannot comprehend anything of God. It is not in God, but external to Him. If we live in Christ, the Spirit of Christ will see through us, and in us. We will see and know what Christ desires.

"Christ dwelling in the soul, causes his light to become a holy substance, a spiritual body, a true temple, in which the Holy Spirit dwells. Selfhood hath not true substance, in which light can be steadfast. It desireth not God's meekness. In meekness and lowliness consisteth the *kingdom* [emphasis added] of heaven. God's substance is humility. He who came to rescue us from the evil power, described himself as 'meek and lowly;' and He could announce, when quit of coarse flesh and blood disguise, that to him was given 'all power in heaven and in earth.' The mysteries of God are revealed to the meek. Let the soul lose no time in trying to clothe itself with humility! Humility is the throne of love; unless this throne is firmly established, love is quickly deposed by every spasm of self-will. It is more blessed to continue under the cross of Christ, in patience and meekness, than to bring down 'fire from heaven!' There is no contention in Christ, but love and humility.

"The flowers of the earth do not grudge at one another, though one be more beautiful and fuller of virtue than another, but they stand humbly, kindly, one by another and enjoy one another's virtues; so we all please God, if we give up ourselves into his will, if standing humbly in His field.

"Our trance of selfishness must end, for we are all being organized, by the one only life, in the one body. In the Body of Christ, self-seeking is a monstrosity! The whole body must be 'fitly joined together and compacted by that which every joint (or joining) supplieth, unto the edifying of itself in love.' The second manifestation of Christ to His people will be in their bodies. Our Lord hath need of each one in His great, mystical body; and they must all be one in Him, the Anointed!

"There is a life, this world comprehendeth it not; it hath no fire to consume, but a mighty fire in light and love and joy; a fire of brightness and majesty, no pain therein. It hath a body without defect, want, misery, anger, death or devil. The Holy Spirit is its air and spirit; it is filled with love and joy. This life has been from eternity uprising and blossoming! It is not of this earth, but substantial,—the eternal life! and all who have received this life, at the end of the age, will be presented pure and without blemish, one body in Christ!

"In the time of the end, the time of the Lily, these writings will be sought as serviceable. To all such who are shooting forth into the fair Lily in the *kingdom* [emphasis added] of God, who are in the process of birth, are these lines written; that each may be strengthened, and bud in the life of God, and grow and bear fruit in the Tree of paradise; that each branch and twig in this fair Tree may contribute, help and shelter all the other branches and twigs, that this Tree may become a great Tree! Then shall we all rejoice, one with another, with joy unspeakable and full of glory."

Chapter 3

Part I

The Passion for Private Places With God

ONCE AGAIN WE SEE PASSION COLLIDING head-on with the prevailing religious thought of the day. This time it is the passion of our Lord for prayer. In the day that Jesus walked the earth, the spiritual life of Israel had reduced prayer to rote public performances of self-righteousness and repetition by the temple leaders. It was empty and devoid of any meaningful communion with the Father.

The leaders used their prayers as a means to exalt themselves, that they might appear pious and holy before men. Oh, the words were expressive and poetic, and spoken with great fervor and intensity, but they were sadly lacking. Such prayers were prayed from empty hearts to an apparent distant God whom they did not know. The Israelites might just as well have been offering up prayers to the Greek gods. Spiritual frauds, these men simply deceived themselves. Even worse, they misled those who followed them. "Whitewashed tombs" is what Jesus likened them to...the blind leading the blind.[1] They had passed on the emptiness of their own experience to a whole nation. Such wanton abuse of the sheep of Israel filled Jesus with wrath!

---

1.   See Matthew 15:14; 23:27.

And Jesus entered the temple and cast out all those who were buying and selling in the temple, and overturned the tables of the moneychangers and the seats of those who were selling doves. And He said to them, "It is written, 'My house shall be called a house of prayer'; but you are making it a robbers' den" (Matthew 21:12-13).

Jesus strode into the house of His Father and found it desecrated by the carnal exploitation of the holy. With holy anger He overthrew the tables of commercialism, passionately declaring, "My Father's house will be called a house of prayer!" The Son was furious to find His Father's house filled with, not prayer, but the vile pursuit of the god of mammon.

And when you pray, you are not to be as the hypocrites; for they love to stand and pray in the synagogues and on the street corners, in order to be seen by men....But you, when you pray, go into your inner room, and ***when you have shut your door, pray to your Father*** *who is in secret, and your Father who sees in secret will repay you* (Matthew 6:5-6).

Jesus stepped into this meaningless cycle of ceremonial ritual as the only "Ascending One." He coveted for this lost people to know the God of their fathers; to breathe in the rarified air where Father dwells; and to taste the sweet communion that He and the Father enjoyed. He ached for their lost heritage. He knew that the pure practice of prayer was their right and privilege—but they didn't know how to pray.

"The laws of God are immutable, including the natural laws of gravity. 'What goes up must come down!' The law of gravity applies here. In the days of Aaron, the incense of prayer created a cloud as the fragrant smoke of the incense covered the mercy seat of the ark of the covenant. Then God would descend and distill His visible qualities in the midst of the cloud where He would commune with the High Priest. The Presence of God always descended *after* the fragrance of prayer ascended."[2]

"Prayer," says Walter Hilton, "is nothing else but an ascending or getting up of the desire of the heart into God by withdrawing it from earthly thoughts." In the same vein, William Law defines

---

2.   Jim W. Goll, *The Lost Art of Intercession* (Shippensburg, Pennsylvania: Revival Press, 1997), 38.

prayer as "the rising of the soul out of the vanity of time into the riches of eternity."[3]

"We ascend," says St. Augustine, "thy ways that be in our heart, and sing a song of degrees; we glow inwardly with thy fire, with thy good fire, and we go, because we go upwards to the peace of Jerusalem."[4]

For Jesus, this ascending prayer was not an addendum or an afterthought to His ministry. It was not what He did when all else failed or as an emergency measure in a crisis. It was not His master key to usher in revival. It was not the program for world evangelism. It was not even a spiritual discipline. How could one call this loving, sweet, intimate communion He enjoyed with Father a *discipline*?

Prayer was His life! Prayer was His strength, His joy, His very breath. *Prayer was His passion.* Like His natural forefather David, Jesus longed for the courts of the Lord. He was homesick for that place where all existed for the pleasure of the Father...where ten thousand times ten thousand angel voices sang out in continuous joyful praises to the Eternal One. Oh, the Presence of Father God!

Jesus began His public ministry in prayer, sustained it with prayer, finished it in prayer, and now sits at the right hand of His Father, still ever praying for His own!

Prayer is shutting ourselves away with God.

The meaning and importance of prayer in our generation have been greatly obscured by our guilt-motivated drive to serve God. We feel pressed to serve in the house of God. We want to take time to pray, we really do! But there are so many needs, so many meetings, and only so many hours in the day. When we do wrench ourselves away to go into our closet, we find our attempts at truly meaningful dialogue with our God to be very awkward. Yet prayer is the only pathway that leads to the Divine Presence of the Father. It leads us, as children, into the living room of the Father. It is a shutting out of the clamor of the world and stepping into a realm where all is God.

---

3.   Richard Foster and James Bryan Smith, eds. *Devotional Classics* (San Francisco, California: Harper Collins, 1990, 1991, 1993 by RENOVARÉ), 112, 113.

4.   Evelyn Underhill, *Mysticism*, 1911. May 27, 1999. October 5, 1999. <http://ccel.wheaton.edu/u/underhill/mysticism/mysticism1.0-MYSTICIS-4.html/>.

"Prayer then means yearning for the simple presence of God, for a personal understanding of his word, for knowledge of his will and for capacity to hear and obey him. It is thus something much more than uttering petitions for good things external to our deepest concerns....we wish to hear His word and respond to it with our whole being."[5]

What a stark contrast this is to the Christian prayers of our day! Our prayers are consumed with our own problems and concerns for our loved ones. We, along with much of the Church down through the corridors of time, have lost the pure, undiluted wonder of moments spent in the Presence of Father. Yet true prayer has always been about shutting one's self away with God. It is "communion and union of man with God, [and] by its actions it upholds the world."[6]

How often we find ourselves in prayer, telling God what we think He should be doing and reminding Him of what is going on in our little world—in case He hadn't noticed. How different were the prayers of the Son!

It was in the presence of the Father that Jesus received His agenda for the day. He never thought of making a decision without the affirmation of His Father. Major confrontations and major victories—such as the selection of the disciples, the deliverance of the disciples at sea, and the healing of a demoniac—always followed on the heels of His times of solitude. In the place of prayer we too can be drawn into something larger than ourselves and discover new dimensions of service to God and man.

If Jesus disappeared, the disciples knew where they could find Him...on the mountain, praying. He had to withdraw from the distractions of the never-ending needs that relentlessly called out to Him in order to maintain His center of quiet, which came from His intimacy with Father. His homesickness for the courts of Father's house could be assuaged only in the place of communion.

"Why should we flounder like tired butterflies in this vast web of ecclesiastical confusion wondering why our heavenly wings still fail to lift us into God's pure air? Most true lovers of the Lord

---

5.   Thomas Merton, *Contemplative Prayer* (New York: Doubleday, 1969, 1996), 67.

6.   St. John of the Ladder, *Desert Father*. 1997. November 30, 1999. <http://users.otenet.gr/~marinarb/prayer.htm/>.

Jesus do at sometime or other escape the web, even if it be for an hour or two, and in some informal way taste the sweetness of His presence...."[7]

If we want to become known on the mountaintop, we must learn to escape the web of ecclesiastical confusion and frenetic activity down on the plains of liturgy and ritualism. We must break free from being slaves to the very schedules we created. We must release ourselves from the addictions of entertainment and earthly enticements that consume huge portions of our time. We must even loose ourselves from the soulish satisfaction we derive from serving God. Only in the solitude of the quiet place will we find our true reason for being: to delight in the Lord our God and to bring pleasure to Him!

"I realised that I was caught in a web of strange paradoxes. While complaining about too many demands, I felt uneasy when none were made. While speaking about the burden of letter writing, an empty mailbox made me sad. While fretting about tiring lecture tours, I felt disappointed when there were no invitations. While speaking nostalgically about an empty desk, I feared the day in which that would come true. In short, while desiring to be alone I was frightened of being left alone. The more I became aware of these paradoxes, the more I started to see how much I had fallen in love with my own compulsions and illusions, and how much I needed to step back and wonder, 'Is there a quiet stream underneath the fluctuating affirmations and rejections of my little world? Is there a still point where my life is anchored and from which I can reach out with hope and courage and confidence?' "[8]

"Solitude is the place where the whole of our personality and being, seen and unseen, is drawn together in the transforming presence of God's love. But more than that the silence of solitude is the silence of eternity. We are drawn into the mystery of something much bigger than ourselves. It places us, with all that he has

7.   Geoffrey Bull, *The Sky Is Red* (Hodder & Stoughton Ltd., 1965; London: Pickering & Inglis, 1981), 168.

8.   Henri Nouwen, *The Genesee Diary*, (Image Books, 1981), 14, as quoted in David Runcorn, *A Center of Quiet* (Downers Grove, Illinois: InterVarsity Press, 1990), 74.

made, in the heart of God's cosmic love and presence. It is there that life is renewed, restored and given its true perspective."[9]

"If our activity and business has been a way of avoiding deeper questions and concerns, then we may feel, for a while at least, as if we are standing in the path of a dam that has burst. We are often so cluttered inside with the accumulation of years—hopes and fears, plans and ideas, light and darkness—that the Holy Spirit has to first of all clear a space. In the Quaker tradition the presence of the Holy Spirit within us is described as 'sifting silence.' It is disturbing to experience it, but this clearing work is deeply loving. Just because we feel in turmoil does not mean that God is too! The neglect of our inner world may mean that a lot of suppressed energy is locked up within us."[10]

Prayer can be possible only if we are willing to do some "housecleaning" in our spirits. The internal disorder of fears, misconceptions, distractions, and hurts too often prevent us from making our way into the quiet place of true fellowship with our Father. As we yield to the Holy Spirit's internal work, He prepares us and ushers us in to enjoy the intimacy we desire with our God.

The words of prayer are developed in the meditations of our hearts.

Jesus' prayers were not for the benefit of men; He did not piously utter prayers to impress people. He had no need to write out His prayers so as not to forget what He wanted to say to His Father. On the contrary, His words gushed up from the wellsprings of His heart—His thoughts; His desires; His hopes; His constant, abiding love for His Father; every beat of His heart. His prayers sprang from His active engagements in life and from the reflective meditations of His heart.

In fact, His prayers were seldom even spoken before men. Most were uttered in the private places where He could find a few hours' peace from the shrieking pain of a world lost and wandering in empty, desolate places. The crowds of people that He came to seek and to save were a constant demand on His Person, and He needed those times of withdrawal with Father more than He needed food and rest.

9. Runcorn, *A Center of Quiet*, 7.
10. Runcorn, *A Center of Quiet*, 16-17.

After He had dismissed them, He went up on a mountainside by Himself to pray... (Matthew 14:23 NIV).

But Jesus often withdrew to lonely places and prayed (Luke 5:16 NIV).

One of those days Jesus went out to a mountainside to pray, and spent the night praying to God (Luke 6:12 NIV).

About eight days after Jesus said this, He took Peter, John and James with Him and went up onto a mountain to pray (Luke 9:28 NIV).

Wouldn't you like to feel the intensity and emotion of His prayer? Let us slip into the Upper Room where He is celebrating the Passover with His disciples and, with bated breath, listen to the Son talk to His Father.

These things Jesus spoke; and lifting up His eyes to heaven, He said, "Father, the hour has come; glorify Thy Son, that the Son may glorify Thee....I glorified Thee on the earth, having accomplished the work which Thou hast given Me to do. And now, glorify Thou Me together with Thyself, Father, with the glory which I had with Thee before the world was....I ask on their behalf; I do not ask on behalf of the world, but of those whom Thou hast given Me; for they are Thine....But now I come to Thee; and these things I speak in the world, that they may have My joy made full in themselves....I do not ask Thee to take them out of the world, but to keep them from the evil one.... I do not ask in behalf of these alone, but for those also who believe in Me through their word....Father, I desire that they also, whom Thou hast given Me, be with Me where I am, in order that they may behold My glory, which Thou hast given Me; for Thou didst love Me before the foundation of the world" (John 17:1-24).

Can you feel the passion, the intimacy? This is communion between the Lover and His Beloved. There is power and unmistakable passion in the words that pour from the lips of our Lord. He is lost in the wonder of that sense of union and complete abandonment that He always finds with His beloved Father.

One is drawn into the intimacy of the moment—the abandonment of the Son into the arms of His Father. As we listen, our hearts cry out to experience that same love and passion in our own prayers. Oh, to know the Father in such intimacy and passion!

Intimacy is the attraction and magnetism of prayer. It is the inherent instinct in all of us that longs for a return to the One who formed us. We are wooed into the place of prayer by the possibility, by the promise, of a *love affair* with the Eternal God. Without true intimacy, prayer is reduced to mere liturgy and mechanical discourse. To call prayer a discipline is to relegate the Lover of our souls to just another obligation we must tend to.

This place of intimate solitude is found in the chambers of our hearts. It is not a matter of looking up, but of looking in where Christ dwells in our hearts. When we do, we will discover Him in the privacy of our thoughts and in the sweetness of our meditations. He is there, and He is not silent.

"Christ comes only in secret to those who have entered the inner chamber of the heart and closed the door behind them."[11]

The disciples were awed by the intimacy of Jesus' prayers. They had years of attending the synagogue and observing the activity of their religious leaders. The prayers and spiritual incantations intoned by these sanctimonious scribes were pious attempts at spiritual dialogue that left the disciples empty and utterly cynical. But Jesus awakened within them a newly found hunger for meaningful communion with the God of Israel. They joyously and wondrously realized, as they observed their Master, that such communion was actually possible. Jolted out of generations of despair, they anxiously entreated Jesus to teach them how to pray.

It is at this point that we must be very careful lest we too slide into the deceptive, humanistic ways of our day. If that question were asked of the preachers of our day, they would pull out their sermons and launch into eloquent dissertations on how to pray. We would get a theological presentation on the importance of prayer, where to pray, keys to prayer, and on and on.

Jesus did not deliver a soliloquy on prayer to His disciples. When Jesus heard them mention the word *prayer*, an explosion of divine energy and joy exploded within Him that came forth in a passionate outpouring of prayer to His Father. He didn't sit them down and explain the principles of prayer. No! Right there, right then, He stepped into that other realm—the realm where Daddy lived—and lovingly drew His disciples with Him.

From His lips poured forth the passions, burdens, and reflections that were buried in His spirit. "Our Father who art in heaven...."[12] What He taught them that day was that the Father was accessible. At any moment, in any place, a conference call could be set up and the "technology" was available to "reach out and touch" the Throne. Heaven's ear was forever poised

---

11. Merton, *Contemplative Prayer*, 56.
12. Matthew 6:9.

to hear the cry of a sincere heart. The disciples did not need anyone to mediate for them. They had to but call out to the Father in simplicity and heartfelt worship. Jesus assured them that God is *"our* Father."

What we believers have done is copied His prayer and made it ours. Why? We have no depth of expression within us. *We borrow the prayers of others because we have no prayer of our own!*

If we are not careful, prayer could end up being the foundation for a new movement or even...should we say it?...a denomination. For Jesus, it was not a new truth to emphasize; it was a way of life. Jesus was attracted to the private places where He could deliver His soul to the Father. We, however, are attracted to the public places where we can demonstrate our righteousness. Jesus was pulled into the presence of His Father where He verbalized His love, while we are drawn to the platforms where we can display our gifts.

Prayer is our refuge from the trials of life.

When confronted with the opposition of man, Jesus did not seek the solace of friends; He sought the seclusion of the Father. In that quiet place He was able to pour out His soul and to wrestle with the challenges before Him. It was in the dwelling places of prayer that He found the consolation of the Father. This was not escapism. In the presence of Father He found the strength to continue with His face set as a flint toward the cross that He knew awaited Him.

Polycarp, a disciple of John, was hotly pursued by the proconsul. He withdrew to a farm where, night and day, as was his habit, he prayed for the Church throughout the world. Polycarp fell into a trance and for three days lived in the presence of his Father. While in that trance, he saw his pillow burning with fire. Immediately he knew that his life would be taken at the fiery stake. When the proconsul's men found him, he persuaded them to grant him an hour that he might pray. For two hours he prayed with great grace and power. Those around him were amazed and repented.

Nevertheless, they returned him to the city where he was burned at the stake. From that stake we can still hear Polycarp's passionate prayer:

"O Lord God Almighty the Father of Thy beloved and blessed Son Jesus Christ, through whom we have received the knowledge of Thee, the God of angels and powers of all creation and of the whole race of the righteous, who live in Thy presence; I bless

Thee for that Thou hast granted me this day and hour, that I might receive a portion amongst the number of martyrs in the cup of (Thy) Christ unto resurrection of eternal life, both of soul and of body, in the incorruptibility of the Holy spirit. May I be received among these in Thy presence this day, as a rich and acceptable sacrifice, as Thou didst prepare and reveal it beforehand, and hast accomplished it, Thou are the faithful and true God. For this cause, yea and for all things, I praise Thee, I bless Thee, I glorify Thee, through the eternal and heavenly High-priest Jesus Christ Thy beloved son, through whom with Him and the Holy Spirit be glory both now (and ever) and for the ages to come. Amen."[13]

The witnesses there that day said that the fire seemed to form a vault around him. Neither did they smell burning flesh, but rather a fragrant odor, as of some precious spice. Thus Polycarp ascended into the arms of his Father.

The private passionate prayer will make way for the triumphant and glorious witness of the public prayer. You cannot pray with strength in public until you have first poured out your soul in private. It is the wrestling with God in prayer in the seclusion of the Garden that gives us the resolve to pray on the cross of our life's trials and testings. No man can courageously embrace the martyrdom of a cross until he has first met with God in the interior places of the heart.

It is in the lonely, dark night of prayer that we listen for the words of the Father that give us courage for the day to come. It is in the silence of the night that we lay hold of the strength for the movements of the day.

13.　J.B. Lightfoot, *The Apostolic Fathers* (Grand Rapids, Michigan: Baker Book House, first printing 1956), 113-114.

Chapter 3

Part II

Concise View of the Way to God; And of The State of Union[1]

Madame Jeanne Guyon was born in 1648 in Montargis, France. At the age of 15 she married an invalid and began a long series of persecutions from her husband's family, church dignitaries, and politicians. "All this because she loved the Lord and lived a holy life; because she served the people with intense self-sacrifice, having the gifts of healing and the discerning of spirits; because she wrote as the Spirit dictated and taught the people the art of communing with God without a prayer book."[2]

*   *   *

Madame Guyon

"And the glory which Thou gavest me, I have given them; that they may be one even as we are one, (I in them and Thou in me,) that they may be made perfect in one."—John xvii. 22.

---

1.   James W. Metcalf, ed. *Spiritual Progress* or *Instructions in the Divine Life of the Soul From the French of Fenelon and Madame Guyon* (New York: M.W. Dodd, 1853). March 25, 1997. August 13, 1999. <http://www.ccel.org/f/fenelon/progress/spirit05.htm/>. Public domain. Reprinted as is.

2.   Abbie C. Morrow, ed. *Sweet Smelling Myrrh* (Salem, Ohio: Schmul Publishing, 1996), 4.

Part I.

ON THE WAY TO GOD

CHAPTER I.

THE FIRST DEGREE: CONVERSION.

1. The first degree is the return of the soul to God, when, being truly converted, it begins to subsist by means of grace.

CHAPTER II.

THE SECOND DEGREE:
THE EFFECTUAL TOUCH IN THE WILL.

2. The soul then receives *an effectual touch in the will*, which invites it to recollection, and instructs it that God is within, and must be sought there; that He is present in the heart, and must be there enjoyed.

3. This discovery, in the beginning, is the source of very great joy to the soul, as it is an intimation or pledge of happiness to come; in its very commencement, the road it is to pursue is opened and is shown to be that of the inward life. This knowledge is the more admirable, as it is the spring of all the felicity of the soul, and the solid foundation of interior progress; for those souls who tend toward God merely by the intellect, even though they should enjoy a somewhat spiritual contemplation, yet can never enter into intimate union, if they do not quit that path and enter this of the inward touch, where the whole working is in the will.

4. Those who are led in this way, though conducted by a blind abandonment, yet experience a savory knowledge. They never walk by the light of the intellect, like the former, who receive distinct lights to guide them, and who, having a clear view of the road, never enter those impenetrable passes of the hidden will which are reserved for the latter. The former proceed upon the evidence furnished by their illuminations, assisted by their reason, and they do well; but the latter are destined to pursue blindly an unknown course, which, nevertheless, appears perfectly natural to them, although they seem obliged to feel their way. They go, however, with more certainty than the others, who are subject to be misled in their intellectual illuminations; but these are guided by a supreme Will which conducts them howsoever it will. And further, all the

more immediate operations are performed in the centre of the soul, that is, in the three powers reduced to the unity of the will, where they are all absorbed, insensibly following the path prescribed for them by that touch to which we have before referred.

5. These latter are they who pursue the way of Faith and absolute Abandonment. They have neither relish nor liberty for any other path; all else constrains and embarrasses them. They dwell in greater aridities than the others, for as there is nothing distinct to which their minds are attached, their thoughts often wander and have nothing to fix them. And as there are differences in souls, some having more sensible delights, and others being drier, so it is with those who are led by the will; the former sort have more relish and less solid acquirement, and should restrain their too eager disposition, and suffer their emotions to pass, even when they seem burning with love; the latter seem harder and more insensible, and their state appears altogether natural; nevertheless, there is a delicate something in the depth of the will, which serves to nourish them, and which is, as it were, the condensed essence of what the others experience in the intellect and in ardor of purpose.

6. Still, as this support is exceedingly delicate, it frequently becomes imperceptible, and is hidden by the slightest thing. This gives rise to great suffering, especially in times of tribulation and temptation; for as the relish and support are delicate and concealed, the will partakes of the same character in a high degree, so that such souls have none of those strong wills. Their state is more indifferent and insensible, and their way more equable; but this does not hinder them from having as severe and even more serious trouble than others; for nothing being done in them by impulse, everything takes place, as it were, naturally, and their feeble, insensible, hidden wills cannot be found, to make head against their foes. Their fidelity, however, often excels that of the others. Notice the striking difference between Peter and John; one seems to be overflowing with extraordinary zeal, and falls away at the voice of a maid-servant; the other makes no external manifestation, and remains faithful unto the end.

7. You will ask me, then, if these souls are urged on by no violent influence, but walk in blindness, do they do the will of God? They do, more truly, although they have no distinct assurance of it; His will is engraved in indelible characters on their very inmost recesses, so that they perform with a cold and languid, but firm and inviolable, abandonment, what the others accomplish by the drawings of an exquisite delight.

8. Thus they go on under the influence of this divine touch, from one degree to another, by a faith more or less sensibly savory, and experience con-

stant alternations of aridity and enjoyment of the presence of God, but ever finding that the enjoyment becomes continually deeper and less perceptible, and thus more delicate and interior. They discover, too, that in the midst of their aridity, and without any distinct illumination, they are not the less enlightened; for this state is luminous in itself, though dark to the soul that dwells in it. And so true is this, that they find themselves more acquainted with the truth; I mean that truth implanted in their interior, and which causes everything to yield to the Will of God. This divine Will becomes more familiar to them, and they are enabled, in their insipid way, to penetrate a thousand mysteries that never could have been discovered by the light of reason and knowledge. They are insensibly and gradually preparing, without being aware of it, for the states that are to follow.

9. The trials of this state are alternations of dryness and facility. The former purified the attachment or tendency and natural relish that we have for the enjoyment of God. So that the whole of this degree is passed in these alternations of enjoyment, aridity, and facility, without any intermixture of temptations, except very transitory ones, or certain faults; for in every state, from the beginning onward, the faults of nature are much more liable to overtake us in times of aridity than in seasons of interior joy, when the unction of grace secures us from a thousand evils. In all the preceding states thus far, the soul is engaged in combatting its evil habits, and in endeavoring to overcome them by all sorts of painful self-denial.

10. In the beginning, when God turned its look inward, he so influenced it against itself, that it was obliged to cut off all its enjoyments, even the most innocent, and to load itself with every kind of affliction. God gives no respite to some in this regard, until the life of Nature, that is, of the exterior senses as manifested in appetites, likes and dislikes, is wholly destroyed.

11. This destruction of the appetites and repugnances of the outward senses, belongs to the second degree, which I have called *the effectual touch in the will*, and in which the highest and greatest virtue is practised, especially when the inward drawing is vigorous and the unction very savory. For there is no sort of contrivance that God does not discover to the soul, to enable it to conquer and overcome self in everything; so that at length, by this constant practice, accompanied by the gracious unction before referred to, the spirit gets the upper hand of nature, and the interior part comes under subjection without resistance. There is, then, no further trouble from this source, any more than if all external feeling had been taken away. This state is mistaken, by those who are but little

enlightened, for a state of death; it is, indeed, the death of the senses, but there is yet a long way to that of the spirit.

CHAPTER III.

THE THIRD DEGREE:
PASSIVITY AND INTERIOR SACRIFICE.

12. When we have for some time enjoyed the repose of a victory that has cost us so much trouble, and suppose ourselves forever relieved from an enemy whose whole power has been destroyed, we enter into the third degree, next in order to the other, which is a way of faith more or less savory, according to the state. We enter into a condition of alternate dryness and facility, as I have stated, and in this dryness, the soul perceives certain exterior weaknesses, natural defects, which, though slight, take it by surprise; it feels, too, that the strength it had received for the struggle, is dying away. This is caused by the loss of our active, inward force; for although the soul, in the second degree, imagines itself to be in silence before God, it is not entirely so. It does not speak, indeed, either in heart or by mouth, but it is in an active striving after God and constant out-breathing of love, so that, being the subject of the most powerful amorous activity, exerted by the Divine Love towards Himself, it is continually leaping, as it were, towards its object, and its activity is accompanied by a delightful and almost constant peace. As it is from this activity of love that we acquire the strength to overcome nature, it is then that we practice the greatest virtues and most severe mortifications.

13. But just in proportion as this activity decays, and is lost in an amorous passivity, so does our strength of resistance sink and diminish, and, as this degree advances, and the soul becomes more and more passive, it becomes more and more powerless in combat. As God becomes strong within, so do we become weak. Some regard this impossibility of resistance as a great temptation, but they do not see that all our labor, aided and assisted by grace, can only accomplish the conquest of our outward senses, after which God takes gradual possession of our interior, and becomes Himself our purifier. And as He required all our watchfulness while He continued us in amorous activity, so He now requires all our fidelity to let Him work, while He begins to render Himself Lord by the subjection of the flesh to the Spirit.

14. For it must be observed that all our outward perfection depends upon, and must follow the inward; so that when we are employed in active devotion, however simple, we are actively engaged against ourselves just as simply.

15. The second degree accomplishes the destruction of the outward senses, the third, that of the inward, and this is brought about by means of this *savory passivity*. But as God is then working within, He seems to neglect the outward, and hence the reappearance of defects, though feebly and only in a time of aridity, which we thought extinct.

16. The nearer we approach the termination of the third degree, the longer and more frequent are our aridities, and the greater our weakness. This is a purification which serves to destroy our internal feelings, as the amorous activity put an end to our external, and in each degree, there are alternations of dryness and enjoyment. The dryness serves as a purifier from its barrenness and weakness. As soon as we cease, from inability, to practice mortifications of our own fashioning, those of Providence take their place—the crosses which God dispenses according to our degree. These are not chosen by the soul; but the soul, under the interior guidance of God, receives such as He appoints.

CHAPTER IV.

THE FOURTH DEGREE: NAKED FAITH.

17. The fourth degree is *naked faith*; here we have nothing but inward and outward desolation; for the one always follows the other.

18. Every degree has its beginning, progress, and consummation.

19. All that has hitherto been granted and acquired with so much labor, is here gradually taken away.

20. This degree is the longest, and only ends with total death, if the soul be willing to be so desolated as to die wholly to self. For there is an infinite number of souls that never pass the first degrees, and of those who reach the present state there are very few in whom its perfect work is accomplished.

21. This desolation takes place in some with violence, and although they suffer more distress than others, yet they have less reason to complain, for the very severity of their affliction is a sort of consolation. There are others who experience only a feebleness and a kind of disgust for everything, which has the appearance of being a failure in duty and unwillingness to obey.

22. We are first deprived of our voluntary works, and become unable to do what we did in the preceding degrees; and as this increases, we begin to feel a general inability in respect to everything, which, instead of diminishing, enlarges day by day. This weakness and inability gradually taking possession of us, we enter upon a condition in which we say: *"For that which I do, I allow not; for what I would, that do I not; but what I hate, that do I."* (Rom. vii. 15.)

23. After being thus deprived of all things, both inward and outward, which are not essential, the work begins upon those which are; and in proportion as the virtuous life becoming a Christian, which we regarded with so much complacency, disappears, we are likewise spoiled of a certain interior delight and substantial support. As this support becomes weaker and more subtile, the more perceptible becomes its loss. It is to be remarked, however, that there is no loss except to our own consciousness, as it still exists in the soul, but imperceptibly and without apparent action. If it were not hidden, the death and loss of self could not be accomplished. But it retires within, and shuts itself up so closely that the soul is not aware of its presence.

24. Do you ask why this course is pursued? The whole object of the way thus far has been to cause the soul to pass from multiplicity to the distinct sensible without multiplicity; from the distinct sensible to the distinct insensible; then to the sensible indistinct, which is a general delight much less attractive than the other. It is vigorous in the beginning and introduces the soul into the perceived, which is a purer and less exquisite pleasure than the first; from the perceived, into faith sustained and working by love; passing in this way from the sensible to the spiritual, and from the spiritual to naked faith, which, causing us to be dead to all spiritual experiences, makes us die to ourselves and pass into God, that we may live henceforth from the life of God only.

25. In the economy of grace, then, we begin with sensible things, continue with those which are spiritual, and end by leading the soul gradually into its centre, and uniting it with God.

26. The more deeply this imperceptible support retires, the more does it knit the soul together, so that it cannot continue to multiply itself among a thousand things which it can no longer either affect or even perceive; and, entirely stripped, it is gradually obliged to desert even itself.

27. It is stripped without mercy, then, equally and at the same time, of everything both within and without, and what is worst of all, is delivered over to temptations; and the more fully it is thus given up to temptation, the more completely is it deprived of strength to resist them from without; thus it is weakened still farther at the very time when it is subjected to more violent attacks, and finally its internal support is removed, which, while it served as a refuse and asylum, would be an evidence of the goodness of God, and of its faithfulness to itself.

28. So you may see a man pursued by a powerful adversary; he fights, and defends himself as well as he is able, always contriving, however, to get nearer and nearer to a stronghold of safety; but the longer he fights the weaker he

becomes, while the strength of his opponent is constantly increasing. What shall he do? He will gain the portal of the stronghold as adroitly as he can, for there he will find abundant aid. But, on reaching it, he sees that it is closed, and finds that, far from rendering him any assistance, the keepers have barricaded every loophole of refuge; he must fall into the hands of his powerful enemy, whom he recognizes, when, defenceless and in despair, he has given himself up, as his best and truest friend.

29. Be sure, then, that this degree comprehends all these things; the privation of every good, the accumulation of all sorts of weaknesses, powerlessness of defence, no interior asylum; God himself often appears angry; and, to crown all, temptations.

30. Willingly, I think I hear you say, provided I might be sure that my will was not in harmony with the malignity of nature and the weaknesses of the senses. Ah! you would be too happy; but that cannot be. In proportion as you become enfeebled and destitute of every operation and activity of love, however insignificant, the will, which was founded in that vigor of love, becoming weaker day by day, gradually disappears; and vanishing thus, it is certain that it takes no part in anything that is passing in the man, but is separate. But as it does not manifest itself anywhere, by any sign, it affords no assured support to the soul, but the contrary; for, no longer finding the will in an attitude of resistance, the soul believes that it is consenting to everything, and that it has joined in with the animal will, which is the only one perceptible.

31. You will, perhaps, remind one that I have before stated that, in the first contest of amorous activity, nature and the senses had become, as it were, extinguished and subdued. It is true; but the spirit of self, by the very victories that grace had thus acquired for it, has become high-minded, more tenacious of what it esteems good, and still more indomitable. God, who is determined to subdue it, makes use for that purpose, of an apparent resurrection of that same nature which the soul supposed dead. But observe that He does not use nature until He has extracted its malignity, destroyed it and separated the superior will from that which rendered it violent and criminal. He extracts the venom of the viper, and then uses it as an antidote to the spirit. Whoever shall become acquainted with the admirable economy of grace and the wisdom of God in bringing man to a *total sacrifice of self*, will be filled with delight, and, insensible as he may be, will expire with love. The little traces of it which have been revealed to my heart, have often overwhelmed me with ecstasy and transport.

32. Fidelity in this degree requires us to suffer spoliation to the whole extent of the designs of God, without being anxious about ourselves, sacrific-

ing to God all our interests both for time and for eternity. Nothing must be made a pretext for reserving or retaining the slightest atom, for the least reservation is the cause of an irreparable loss, as it prevents our death, from being total. We must let God work his absolute pleasure, and suffer the winds and tempests to beat upon us from every quarter, submerged, as we may often be, beneath the tumultuous billows.

33. A wonderful thing is here perceived; far from being estranged by our suffering and wretched state, it is then that God appears; and if any weakness has been apparent, He gives us some token of his immediate presence, as if to assure the soul for a moment, that He was with it in its tribulation. I say *for a moment*, for it is of no service subsequently, as a support, but is rather intended to point out the way and invite the soul to the further loss of self.

34. These states are not continuous in their violence; there are remissions, which, while they afford space for taking breath, serve, at the same time, to render the subsequent trial more painful. For nature will make use of anything to sustain its life, as a drowning man will support himself in the water by clinging to the blade of a razor, without adverting to the pain it causes him, if there be nothing else within his reach.

CHAPTER V.

THE FIFTH DEGREE: MYSTICAL DEATH.

35. Attacked thus on all sides by so many enemies, without life and without support, we have no resource but to expire in the arms of Love. When death is complete, the most terrible states cause no further trouble. We do not recognize death from the fact of having passed through all these states, but by an absolute want of power to feel pain, to think of or care for self, and, by our indifference to remaining there forever, without manifesting the slightest sign of vitality. Life is evidenced by a will for or repugnance to something; but here, in this death of the soul, all things are alike. It remains dead and insensible to everything that concerns itself, and, let God reduce it to what extremity He will, feels no repugnance. It has no choice between being Angel or Demon, because it has no longer any eyes for self. It is then that God has placed all its enemies beneath his footstool, and, reigning supreme, takes and possesses it the more fully, as it has the more completely deserted itself. But this takes place by degrees.

36. There remains for a long time, even after death, a trace of the living heat, which is only gradually dissipated. All states effect somewhat towards cleansing the soul, but here the process is completed.

37. We do not die spiritually, once for all, as we do naturally; it is accomplished gradually; we vibrate between life and death, being sometimes in one and sometimes in the other, until death has finally conquered life. And so it is in the resurrection; an alternate state of life and death, until life has finally overcome death.

38. Not that the new life does not come suddenly. He who was dead, finds himself living, and can never afterward doubt that he was dead and is alive again; but it is not then established; it is rather a disposition toward living, then a settled state of life.

39. The first life of grace began in the sensible, and sank continually inward toward the centre, until, having reduced the soul to unity, it caused it to expire in the arms of love; for all experience this death, but each by means peculiar to himself. But the life that is now communicated arises from within; it is, as it were, a living germ which has always existed there, though unobserved, and which demonstrates that the life of grace has never been wholly absent, however it may have been suffered to remain hidden. There it remained even in the midst of death; nor was it less death because life was concealed in it; as the silk-worm lies long dead in the chrysalis, but contains a germ of life that awakes it to a resurrection. This new life, then, buds in the centre, and grows from there; thence it gradually extends over all the faculties and senses, impregnating them with its own life and fecundity.

40. The soul, endued with this vitality, experiences an infinite contentment; not in itself, but in God; and this especially when the life is well advanced.

41. But, before entering upon the effects of this admirable life, let me say, that there are some who do not pass through these painful deaths; they only experience a mortal languor and fainting, which annihilate them, and cause them to die to all.

42. Many spiritual persons have given the name of death, to the earlier purifications, which are, indeed, a death in relation to the life communicated, but not a total death. They result in an extinguishment of some one of the lives of nature, or of grace; but that is widely different from a general extinction of all life.

43. Death has various names, according to our different manner of expression or conception. It is called a *departure*, that is, a separation from self in

order that we may pass into God; a *loss*, total and entire, of the will of the creature, which causes the soul to be wanting to itself, that it may exist only in God. Now, as this will is in everything that subsists in the creature, however good and holy it may be, all these things must necessarily be destroyed, so far as they so subsist, and so far as the good will of man is in them, that the will of God alone may remain. Everything born of the will of the flesh and the will of man, must be destroyed. Then nothing but the will of God is left, which becomes the principle of the new life, and, gradually animating the old extinguished will, takes its place and changes it into faith.

44. From the time that the soul expires mystically, it is separated generally from everything that would be an obstacle to its perfect union with God; but it is not, for all that, received into God. This causes it the most extreme suffering. You will object here, that, if it be wholly dead, it can no longer suffer. Let me explain.

45. The soul is dead as soon as it is separated from self; but this death or mystic decease is not complete until it has passed into God. Until then, it suffers very greatly, but its suffering is general and indistinct, and proceeds solely from the fact that it is not yet established in its proper place.

46. The suffering which precedes death, is caused by our repugnance to the means that are to produce it. This repugnance to the means whenever these means recur, or grow sharper; but in proportion as we die we become more and more insensible, and seem to harden under the blows, until at last death comes in truth through an entire cessation of all life. God has unrelentingly pursued our life into all its covert hiding places; for so malignant is it, that when hard pressed, it fortifies itself in its refuges, and makes use of the holiest and most reasonable pretexts for existence; but, being persecuted and followed into its last retreat, in a few souls (alas! how few!) it is obliged to abandon them altogether.

47. No pain then remains arising from the means which have caused our death, and which are exactly the opposite to those which used to maintain our life; the more reasonable and holy the latter are in appearance, the more unreasonable and defiled is the look of the other.

48. But after death—which is the cause of the soul's departure from self, that is, of its losing every self-appropriation whatever; for we never know how strongly we cling to objects until they are taken away, and he who thinks that he is attached to nothing, is frequently grandly mistaken, being bound to a thousand things, unknown to himself—after death, I repeat, the soul is entirely rid of self, but not at first received into God. There still exists a something, I know

not exactly what, a form, a human remnant; but that also vanishes. It is a tarnish which is destroyed by a general, indistinct suffering, having no relation to the means of death, since they are passed away and completed; but it is an uneasiness arising from the fact of being turned out of self, without being received into its great Original. The soul loses all possession of self, without which it could never be united to God; but it is only gradually that it becomes fully possessed of Him by means of the new life, which is wholly divine.

CHAPTER VI.

UNION WITH GOD: BUT NOT YET RECOGNIZED.

49. As soon as the soul has died in the embraces of the Lord, it is united to Him in truth and without any intermediate; for in losing everything, even its best possessions, it has lost the means and intermediates which dwelt in them; and even these greatest treasures themselves were but intermediates. It is, then, from that moment, united to God immediately, but it does not recognize it, nor does it enjoy the fruits of its union, until He animates it and becomes its vivifying principle. A bride fainting in the arms of her husband, is closely united to him, but she does not enjoy the blessedness of the union, and may even be unconscious of it; but when he has contemplated her for some time, fainting from excess of love, and recalls her to life by his tender caresses, then she perceives that she is in possession of him whom her soul loves, and that she is possessed by him.

PART II.

ON UNION WITH GOD.

CHAPTER I.

THE RESURRECTION.

50. The soul thus possessed of God, finds that He is so perfectly Lord over it, that it can no longer do anything but what He pleases and as He pleases; and this state goes on increasing. Its powerlessness is no longer painful but pleasant, because it is full of the life and power of the Divine Will.

51. The dead soul is in union, but it does not enjoy the fruits of it until the moment of its *resurrection*, when God, causing it to pass into Him, gives it such

pledges and assurances of the consummation of its divine marriage, that it can no longer doubt: for this immediate union is so spiritual, so refined, so divine, so intimate, that it is equally impossible for the soul to conceive or to doubt it. For we may observe that the whole way whereof we speak, is infinitely removed from any imagination; these souls are not in the least imaginative, having nothing in the intellect, and are perfectly protected from deceptions and illusions, as everything takes place within.

52. During their passage through the way of faith, they had nothing distinct, far distinctness is entirely opposed to faith, and they could not enjoy anything of that sort, having only a certain generality as a foundation upon which everything was communicated to them. But it is far otherwise when the life becomes advanced in God; for though they have nothing distinct for themselves, they have for others, and their illumination for the use of others, though not always received by those for whom it was intended, is the more certain as it is more immediate, and as it were natural.

53. When God raises a soul, that is to say, receives it into Himself, and the living germ, which is no other than the Life and Spirit of the Word, begins to appear, it constitutes *the revelation in it of Jesus Christ*, (Gal. i. 16,) who lives in us by the loss of the life of Adam subsisting in self.

54. The soul is thus received into God, and is there gradually changed and transformed into Him, as food is transformed into the one who has partaken of it. All this takes place without any loss of its own individual existence, as has been elsewhere explained.

55. When transformation begins, it is called *annihilation*, since in changing our form, we become annihilated as to our own, in order to take on His. This operation goes on constantly during life, changing the soul more and more into God, and conferring upon it a continually increasing participation in the divine qualities, making it unchangeable, immovable, etc. But He also renders it fruitful in, and not out of, Himself.

56. This fruitfulness extends to certain persons whom God gives and attaches to the soul, communicating to it his Love, full of Charity. For the love of these divine souls for the persons thus bestowed upon them, while it is far removed from the natural feelings, is infinitely stronger than the love of parents for their children, and though it appears eager and precipitate, it is not so, because he, who exhibits it, merely follows the movement impressed upon him.

57. To make this intelligible, we must know that God did not deprive the senses and faculties of their life, to leave them dead; for though there might be life in the centre of the soul, they would remain dead if that life were not also

communicated to them. It increases by degrees, animates all the powers and senses which, until then, had remained barren and unfruitful, enlarges them in proportion to its communication, and renders them active, but with an activity derived and regulated from God, according to his own designs. Persons in a dying or dead condition, must not condemn the activity of such souls, for they could never have been put in divine motion if they had not passed through the most wonderful death. During the whole period of faith, the soul remains motionless; but after God has infused into it the divine activity, its sphere is vastly extended; but, great as it may be, it cannot execute a self-originated movement.

CHAPTER II.

THE LIFE IN GOD.

58. There is no more to be said here of degrees; that of glory being all that remains, every means being left behind, and the future consisting in our enjoying an infinite stretch of life, and that more and more abundantly. (John x. 10.) As God transforms the soul into Himself, his life is communicated to it more plentifully. The love of God for the creature is incomprehensible, and his assiduity inexplicable; some souls He pursues without intermission, prevents them, seats Himself at their door, and delights Himself in being with them and in loading them with the marks of his love. He impresses this chaste, pure, and tender love upon the heart. St. Paul and St. John the Evangelist, felt the most of this maternal affection. But to be as I have described it, it must be bestowed upon the soul in the state of grace of which I have just spoken; otherwise, such emotions are purely natural.

59. The prayer of the state of faith is an absolute silence of all the powers of the soul, and a cessation of every working, however delicate, especially toward its termination. The soul in that state, perceiving no more prayer, and not being able to set apart fixed seasons for it, since all such exercises are taken away, is led to think that it has absolutely lost all kind of devotion. But when life returns, prayer returns with it, and accompanied by a marvellous facility; and as God takes possession of the senses and faculties, its devotion becomes sweet, gentle, and very spiritual, but always to God. Its former devotion caused it to sink within itself, that it might enjoy God, but that which it now has, draws it out of self, that it may be more and more lost and changed in God.

60. This difference is quite remarkable, and can only be accomplished by experience. The soul is silent in the state of death, but its stillness is barren, and accompanied by a frantic rambling, which leaves no mark of silence save the impossibility of addressing God, either with the lips or the heart. But after the resurrection, its silence is fruitful and attended by an exceedingly pure and refined unction, which is deliciously diffused over the senses, but with such a purity, that it occasions no stay and contracts no taint.

61. It is now impossible for the soul to take what it has not, or to put off what it has. It receives with passive willingness whatever impressions are made upon it. Its state, however overwhelming, would be free from suffering, if God, who moves it towards certain free things, gave them the necessary correspondence. But as their state will not bear it, it becomes necessary that what God wills they should have, should be communicated by means of suffering for them.

62. It would be wrong for such persons to say that they do not wish these means; that they desire God only. He is anxious that they should die to a certain interior support of self, which causes them to say that they desire God only, and if they were to reject these means, they would withdraw themselves from the order of God, and arrest their progress. But, being given simply as means, though fruitful in grace and virtue, however secret and concealed, they finally disappear when the soul finds itself united with the means in God, and He communicates Himself directly. Then God withdraws the means, upon which he no longer impresses any movement in the direction of the person to whom they are attached; because it might then serve as a stay, its utility being at least recognized. The soul can then no longer have what it had, and remains in its first death in respect to them, though still very closely united.

63. In this state of resurrection comes that ineffable silence, by which we not only subsist in God, but commune with Him, and which, in a soul thus dead to its own working, and general and fundamental self-appropriation, becomes a flux and reflux of divine communion, with nothing to sully its purity; for there is nothing to hinder it.

64. The soul then becomes a partaker of the ineffable communion of the Trinity, where the Father of spirits imparts his spiritual fecundity, and makes it one spirit with Himself. Here it is that it communes with other souls, if they are sufficiently pure to receive its communications in silence, according to their degree and state; here, that the ineffable secrets are revealed, not by a momentary illumination, but in God himself, where they are all hid, the soul not possessing them for itself, nor being ignorant of them.

65. Although I have said that the soul then has something distinct, yet it is not distinct in reference to itself, but to those with whom it communes; for what it says is said naturally and without attention, but seems extraordinary to the hearers, who, not finding the thing in themselves, notwithstanding it may be there, consider it as something distinct and wonderful, or perhaps fanatical. Souls that are still dwelling among the gifts, have distinct and momentary illuminations, but these latter have only a general illumination, without defined beams, which is God himself; whence they draw whatever they need, which is distinct whenever it is required by those with whom they are conversing, and without any of it remaining with themselves afterwards.

CHAPTER III.

THE TRANSFORMATION.

66. There are a thousand things that might be said about the inward and celestial life of the soul thus full of life in God, which He dearly cherishes for Himself, and which He covers externally with abasement, because He is a jealous God. But it would require a volume, and I have only to fulfill your request. God is the life and soul of this soul, which thus uninterruptedly lives in God, as a fish in the sea, in inexpressible happiness, though loaded with the sufferings which God lays upon it for others.

67. It has become so simple, especially when its transformation is for advanced, that it goes its way perpetually without a thought for any creature or for itself. It has but one object, to do the will of God. But as it has to do with many of the creatures who cannot attain to this state, some of them cause it suffering by endeavoring to compel it to have a care for self, to take precautions, and so on, which it cannot do; and others by their want of correspondence to the Will of God.

68. The crosses of such souls are the most severe, and God keeps them under the most abject humiliations and a very common and feeble exterior, though they are his delight. Then Jesus Christ communicates Himself in all his states, and the soul is clothed upon both with his inclinations and sufferings. It understands what man has cost Him, what his faithlessness has made Him suffer, what is the redemption of Jesus Christ, and how He has borne his children.

69. The transformation is recognized by the want of distinction between God and the soul, it not being able any longer to separate itself from God; everything is equally God, because it has passed into its Original Source, is

reunited to its ALL, and changed into Him. But it is enough for me to sketch the general outlines of what you desire to know; experience will teach you the rest, and having shown you what I ought to be to you, you may judge of what I am in our Lord.

70. In proportion as its transformation is perfected, the soul finds a more extended quality in itself. Everything is expanded and dilated, God making it a partaker of his infinity; so that it often finds itself immense, and the whole earth appears but as a point in comparison with this wonderful breadth and extension. Whatever is in the order and will of God, expands it; everything else contracts it; and this contraction restrains it from passing out. As the will is the means of effecting the transformation, and the center is nothing else but all the faculties united in the will, the more the soul is transformed, the more its will is changed and passed into that of God, and the more God himself wills for the soul. The soul acts and works in this divine will, which is thus substituted for its own, so naturally, that it cannot tell whether the will of the soul is become the will of God, or the will of God become the will of the soul.

71. God frequently exacts strange sacrifices from souls thus transformed in Him; but it costs them nothing, for they will sacrifice everything to Him without repugnance. The smaller sacrifices cost the most, and the greater ones the least, for they are not required until the soul is in a state to grant them without difficulty, to which it has a natural tendency. This is what is said of Jesus Christ on his coming into the world; "*Then said I, Lo, I come: in the volume of the book it is written of me; I delight to do thy will, O my God; yea, thy love is within my heart.*" (Psalm xi. 7,8.) As soon as Christ comes into any soul to become its living principle, He says the same thing of it; He becomes the eternal Priest who unceasingly fulfills within the soul his sacerdotal office. This is sublime indeed, and continues until the victim is carried to glory.

72. God destines these souls for the assistance of others in the most tangled paths; for, having no longer any anxiety in regard to themselves, nor anything to lose, God can use them to bring others into the way of his pure, naked and assured will. Those who are still self-possessed, could not be used for this purpose; for, not having yet entered into a state where they follow the *will of God blindly* for themselves, but always mingling it with their own reasonings, and false wisdom, they are not by any means in a condition to withhold nothing in following it blindly for others. When I say *withhold nothing*, I mean of that which God desires in the present moment; for He frequently does not permit us to point out to a person all that hinders him, and what we see must come

to pass in respect to him, except in general terms, because he cannot bear it. And though we may sometimes say hard things, as Christ did to the Capernaites, He nevertheless bestows a secret strength to bear it; at least He does so to the souls whom He has chosen solely for Himself; and this is the touchstone.

Chapter 4

Part I

The Passion for Human Trust

JESUS LEADS PETER, JAMES, AND JOHN down from the mountain of glorious encounter into the valley of man's bondage and despair. After breathing the fresh winds of Heaven's sweet fragrance, He must now let His lungs be filled with the bitter stench of the misery of earth's enslaved masses. When they reach the foot of the mountain, Jesus is immediately confronted with His own disciples' faithless attempt to heal a demon-possessed child. Frustrated by their deficiency in faith, they turn to the Master and ask Him why they had failed. Jesus declares to His disciples and to future generations of the redeemed community that faith is the master key that unlocks the door to Heaven's great power.

The Jewish nation was birthed from the womb of faith. Genesis 15:6 says that Abraham believed in God. He had faith. The Hebrew word for "believe," *aman,* means full and complete trusting. "It was not primarily in God's words that he believed, but in God Himself."[1]

---

1.   W.E. Vine, Merrill F. Unger, and William White, Jr., *Vine's Complete Expository Dictionary of Old and New Testament Words* (Nashville, Tennessee: Thomas Nelson, 1985), 16.

This word is akin to the adverb form *amen*, meaning "so be it."[2] Abraham, the father of faith, trusted in Yahweh with his whole being and so ordered his life according to the word of Yahweh. Abraham did not allow his mind to wrestle with the illogical and seemingly impossible implications of that word. He chose to be guided by his heart, which trusted in his God, rather than by his perceptions of reality.

> "He responded with the entirety of his being to the articulated thrust of the divine presence. He had no tangible or visible evidence; indeed, fragments of other ancient traditions woven into the final form of narrative indicate that although his faith never wavered he made repeated attempts to receive a confirmation of his certitude. Nevertheless, he firmly maintained his acceptance of the word. This is not an intellectual assent to a propositional truth. It is the insertion of the wholeness of one's personality into a relation of total openness toward the reality of God."[3]

Throughout the Old Testament, faith would be understood to be obedience to the voice of this mysterious God, the Faceless One. For the most part faith would elude the Jewish people as a nation. They would scorn the voice of the Almighty and shun His precepts. Faith would all but disappear from the face of the earth, except for a remnant that would remain faithful to the one true God, waiting in hope for the promised Messiah.

Jesus initiated His ministry by passionately searching for that remnant of believing ones. When He came down from the mountain after delivering His first great sermon, a Roman centurion confronted Him and entreated Him to come heal his servant, who suffered with a horrible paralysis. As the Lord turned to go to his home, the centurion then stopped the Son of Man in His tracks with a declaration of faith that resounds through the ages. "Lord, I am not worthy for You to come under my roof, but just say the word, and my servant will be healed."[4] If the Lord would only speak the word, his servant would be healed.

Enfolded in a moment of unadulterated joy, Jesus, looking deep into this man's heart, realizes that He has found one of those believing ones. "Now when Jesus heard this, He marveled, and said to those who were

---

2. Vine, Unger, and White, *Vine's*, 17.
3. Samuel Terrien, *The Elusive Presence* (New York: Harper & Row, 1978), 77.
4. Matthew 8:8.

following, 'Truly I say to you, I have not found such great faith with any-one in Israel.' "[5]

"I have not found such great faith with anyone in Israel...." Yes, the Lord had set out on a determined quest to find those who had preserved the ancient faith in His Father. Amongst the afflicted and suffering ones of Israel, He would, indeed, find those who had waited in hope for His appear-ing. They awaited the One who would speak the word that would release the seed of faith they had been nurturing in their hearts.

"He has come to us in His matchless incognito. He is known to faith alone."[6]

The Voice is the key to unlocking faith.

This was the key for releasing Heaven's power: the voice and the faith. On the mountain, where Jesus unveiled His eternal glory, the Voice spoke out of the cloud. The words of the Almighty echoed across the mountain ranges with these words: "This is My beloved Son, with whom I am well-pleased; listen to Him!"[7] Once more moving through the valley of human suffering, the beloved Son announces that if one has faith as a tiny grain of mustard seed, he will be able to move mountains.[8] You see, the unveiled glory of God prepares the surrounding environment for the thun-derous casting of God's word. That word then sets the stage for the eman-cipation of the faith that has been shackled in the hearts of men.

George Soltau put it this way:

"Do we know the voice? Can we be led by the voice? Have we the faith that can follow when the path seems so strangely crooked? There must be such a clear conception of the Lord, together with the cultivated habit of recognizing His gentlest intimation, and obeying it without question. It is a splendid abandonment to the will of another, which has been called a 'holy recklessness', as to consequences. It may oppose human reason and circumstances, but if He calls—FOLLOW—...."[9]

---

5.   Matthew 8:10.
6.   Geoffrey Bull, *The Sky Is Red* (Hodder & Stoughton Ltd., 1965; London: Pickering & Inglis, 1981), 98.
7.   Matthew 17:5.
8.   See Matthew 17:20.
9.   Bull, *The Sky Is Red*, 146.

Mary stands out in the New Testament as a shining example of someone who understood the power resident in her Son. John 2:1 says that "on the third day there was a wedding"; it is this event that initiates the miracle-working ministry of the Lord on the earth. It is surrounded in prophetic realism. The third day is the spiritual symbol of God's day. It is the day of *all God*, when God does His work and man rests. It is the day of resurrection and the time of God's holy Presence.

On the third day a problem arises that promises to ruin the festivity of the marriage—the wine has run out. (We will resist the temptation to delve into the prophetic significance of this passage as we focus on the central thought.) In the midst of the panic of embarrassment and insult to the guests, Mary releases the faith that she has quietly nurtured in her mother's heart; she directs the servants to Jesus and commands them to do whatever He says. By that action, she put herself and the credibility of her untested Son on the line. That was faith! In quiet confidence of the unseen, the person possessed of faith lays his impossibility at the feet of the One who is the Word, then waits in expectation.

Faith is the proper—really, it's the only—response to the Word that is spoken from Heaven. The heart's anticipation requires an action of affirmation. Listen to the words of the prophet Jeremiah: "But he who has stood in the council of the LORD, and has seen, and has heard His word— he who has listened to His word must obey."[10]

Emphasizing the same point, the apostle Paul says in Romans 10:17 that faith comes from hearing, and hearing by the Word of God. Literally that reads, "Then faith is of hearing, and hearing through a word of God."[11]

Faith needs a focus. The Voice of God is that focus. The Voice stimulates the spirit, creating the response that we call faith. That Voice is imperative to the true operation of faith. The cripple will remain at the pool of Bethesda unless the Voice is heard. The demoniac continues to roam the mountainside, tormented by evil spirits, until the Voice roars forth from the mouth of God. The adulteress remains in her bondage to sin and at the mercy of spiteful religious men until the Word exposes their sin and sets her free.

---

10. Jeremiah 23:18, The Jerusalem Bible (Philadelphia, Pennsylvania: Jewish Publication Society, 1985).

11. Jay Green, *Interlinear Greek-English New Testament* (Grand Rapids, Michigan: Baker Book House, 1980), 497.

In an effort to help men understand this spiritual law, Jesus related this parable: "Therefore everyone who hears these words of Mine, and acts upon them, may be compared to a wise man, who built his house upon the rock."[12]

"Hears these words"—The utterance of God's Word is the beginning point for faith.

"Acts upon them"—This is faith's response. Faith is the action that is created by the Word of God. To act without the Voice is to take a false step of presumption. Faith needs the foundation of the spoken word.

The Lord was on a passionate search for human faith.

Jesus, led by the Spirit, walked the dusty paths of Israel ever seeking out the fertile soil of hearts in whom a seed of faith lay buried, waiting for the Giver of Life. The Divine Life within Him earnestly hungered for those encounters. Whenever He *happened* upon a deposit of faith, He spoke words that reverberated through the chambers of the heart in which it lay dormant. That faith, recognizing the Voice of Heaven's authority, would then come bursting forth in a harvest of eternal fruit.

And behold, they were bringing to Him a paralytic, lying on a bed; and ***Jesus seeing their faith*** *said to the paralytic, "Take courage, My son, your sins are forgiven"* (Matthew 9:2).

*Then He touched their eyes, saying, "Be it done to you **according to your faith**"* (Matthew 9:29).

*Then Jesus answered and said to her, "O woman, **your faith is great**; be it done for you as you wish." And her daughter was healed at once* (Matthew 15:28).

One can feel His grieved disappointment when He encounters timidity, fear, and unbelief where He had hoped to find confident faith. In the midst of a horrible storm the disciples shake their Master out of a much-needed sleep, crying out to Him in their fear of being at the mercy of the elements. Wiping the sleep from His eyes, Jesus stands up in the boat instantly aware of the desperate situation they are in. The winds are howling with such force that they have to yell to hear each other. The rain is beating upon their bodies with painful intensity. The waves are pounding upon the small wooden fishing boat, threatening to capsize it at any moment. The

---

12.   Matthew 7:24.

disciples, their ashen faces filled with abject fear, are laying hold of Him, desperately seeking for solace and deliverance. They are totally paralyzed with fear. Not one miracle that they had witnessed their Master perform gives them solace in this life-threatening moment.

*And He said to them, "Why are you timid, you men of **little faith?**"*
Then He arose, and rebuked the winds and the sea; and it became per-
fectly calm (Matthew 8:26).

Many times Jesus had demonstrated before His disciples the awesome authority and supernatural power that was His. Yet again and again He was pained by their lack of understanding of who He was and by the pitifully puny deposit of faith they exhibited when confronted by problematic situations. It was His unwavering faith in Father's ability to keep that which He entrusted to Him that kept the Son from losing heart.

Jesus now stands up in that rocking boat and in righteous anger rebukes the very forces of nature itself. To the utter amazement of these men who had walked so many days with Him and seen so many miracles performed as though they were of no momentous import, the ferocious roar of the storm quiets to a contented purr. After all this time of witnessing all Jesus' divine acts, they still marvel, saying, "What kind of a man is this, that even the winds and the sea obey Him?"[13]

His ultimate intention was not to pridefully parade His Divine power before them yet once again. Rather, He was passionately seeking to lead them down the path of internal deliberation, with the hope that they would arrive at the gate of spiritual revelation. There they would, by the power vested in them by that revelation, do greater deeds than they witnessed Him do. This was the overriding aspiration of His heart—that they themselves would tap into the endless resources that were their heritage.

God is the source of all faith.

"And Jesus answered saying to them, 'Have faith in God.' "[14] The literal rendering of that verse is, "*Have faith of God.*"[15]

Herein lies the real problem to faith. Man struggles in the realm of flesh to try and manufacture faith that does not exist. You cannot experience

---

13. Matthew 8:27.
14. Mark 11:22.
15. Green, *Interlinear Greek-English New Testament*, 148.

God-faith through soulish processes. It cannot be brought into reality through the control of sound doctrine or the coercion of strong determination. Your doctrine can be right and your resolve can be tenacious, but until you have an encounter with God, there can be no faith.

Belief must never be confused with faith. Your doctrine can be correct and you can repeat the tenets of that doctrine like a mantra, but it still will not bring you into faith. You can believe in the words of the Bible and still not trust God. We can quote our Scriptures and recite our creeds with great conviction and still not possess the faith that moves us out of the natural realm and into the supernatural.

Trying to will something into existence is not faith. You can say, "I am healed. I am healed. *I am healed!*", and still not be able to get out of bed. Faith does act—but faith does not come *from* the act. *The act comes from the faith.* Positive confession is not the kind of faith that the Son of Man is looking for, the kind that taps Heaven's inexhaustible resources. It is a Divine Word, a heavenly touch, an encounter with Heaven that ignites faith, that produces a passion of conviction and resignation to the Divine Will and purpose.

Faith can never be attained or produced by the ingenuity or efforts of the human mind and will. It is the faith of God. There is a big difference between the faith of man in God and the faith that God gives to the man of God.

> "Thou seest then, saith he, *that faith is from above from the Lord* [emphasis added], and has great power; but doublemindedness is an earthly spirit from the devil and hath no power. Do thou therefore serve that faith that hath power."[16]

The religious community of Jesus' day was bound up in its own human effort and strict religious beliefs. Because of their spiritual pride, men could not reach out in faith to the Son of Man. Therefore they never experienced the power of faith, because faith is born in the cradle of despair and humility. Only when man recognizes his own need and realizes that the Master is the answer is a cry of faith birthed in him. Notice the desperate cry of those who reach out in faith to the Lord.

---

16. J.B. Lightfoot, "The Shepherd of Hermas," *The Apostolic Fathers* (Grand Rapids, Michigan: Baker Book House, first printing 1956), 191-192.

And behold, a Canaanite woman came out from that region, and began to cry out, saying, "Have mercy on me, O Lord, Son of David; my daughter is cruelly demon-possessed" (Matthew 15:22).

And when he heard that it was Jesus the Nazarene, he began to cry out and say, "Jesus, Son of David, have mercy on me!" (Mark 10:47)

Unfortunately, our spiritual successes often diminish the human cry within us. The cry of faith is often silenced by the confidence that previous spiritual victories produce. Or that cry gets transformed into a subtle boasting in our flesh. We begin to look at these achievements as consequences of our faith, while in truth they may be only the results of human zeal and triumph.

The Father has His own ways of bringing us back to the way of faith and restoring the cry that resurrects trust in God. God is raising up a generation of men and women who have been exposed to their own inadequacies. They have walked into the valley of darkness and despair and been liberated from self-confidence and boastful pride. They have exited from the "dark night of the soul" with a simple faith and trust in their God.

"Therefore, O spiritual soul, when thou seest thy desire obscured, thy affections arid and constrained, and thy faculties bereft of their capacity for any interior exercise, be not afflicted by this, but rather consider it a great happiness, since God is freeing thee from thyself and taking the matter from thy hands. For with those hands, howsoever well they may serve thee, thou wouldst never labour so effectively, so perfectly and so securely (because of their clumsiness and uncleanness) as now, *when God takes thy hand and guides thee in the darkness, as though thou wert blind, to an end and by a way which thou knowest not* [emphasis added]. Nor couldst thou ever hope to travel with the aid of thine own eyes and feet, howsoever good thou be as a walker."[17]

The Son returns looking for faith.

"I tell you that He will bring about justice for them speedily. However, when the Son of Man comes, will He find faith on the earth?" And He

17. St. John of the Cross, *The Dark Night of the Soul*, II, xvi, 7. May 27, 1999. October 7, 1999. <http://ccel.wheaton.edu/j/john of the cross/dark night/dark night bod0.9.html#RTFToC83/>.

also told this parable to certain ones who trusted in themselves that they were righteous, and viewed others with contempt (Luke 18:8-9).

When the Son of Man returns, the Church will eagerly want to impress her Bridegroom with the glories of all that she has done. Joyfully, she will want to display the beauty of all that she has accomplished. Let us step into the future as the Bride takes her Lover by the hand to show Him her works.

We start with the elaborate sanctuaries and edifices. We are confident that He will be awed at the sacrifice and finances that made possible the incredible task of building these ornate structures. We can proudly show the Master that we are no longer the source of ridicule because of our plain and paltry storefront churches.

We continue the tour as we step inside and listen to the swelling sound of music and watch the pomp and circumstance that parades across these oh-so-large, grand platforms. Doesn't the choir look elegant in their robes, and doesn't the music sound majestic and professional? After all, we have the best sound system that money can buy and we have the best musicians that we can hire to make full use of those elite systems. We are sure that the Lord must be impressed at all we have done for *His* glory.

And programs...we have programs. We have programs for the youth, programs for the singles, programs for the divorced, programs for the elderly, and on and on. We have discipleship groups, dance groups, care groups, youth groups, and prayer groups. We have programs on the local radio, our services are recorded for national TV, and of course we have our own Internet site. Yes, we are pretty impressive in our doing the work of the Lord.

When we turn to look at the Lord, we are unprepared for the look of immense sadness that covers His face. We thought that all this would please Him! Were we wrong? He seems to be looking beyond all the things that have given us such great pride and satisfaction. He moves slowly past us and looks around and sees only the *wood, hay, and stubble of a man-made religion.*

When He comes, He will not look for the great things we have built. Rather, as in the beginning, He will look for faith. Where are the believing ones? Where are those who trust in Him? Where are the ones waiting for the sound of His voice? Where are the great acts of sacrificial faith?

Who will rise up in passionate faith, lay hold of the great truths of the Kingdom, and bring down the religious orders of our day?

May this generation produce its own heroes of faith!

And without faith it is impossible to please Him, for he who comes to God must believe that He is, and that He is a rewarder of those who seek Him (Hebrews 11:6).

When He comes, will He find faith on the earth?

Chapter 4

Part II

The Real Faith[1]

The Real Faith by Charles Price is considered to be the classic book on faith. Thousands have been changed by its truths. The simplicity of its message has inspired many to pursue this passion of our Lord. May it birth that passion within your hungry heart as well.

*   *   *

Charles S. Price

The Origins of Faith

I have a very decided dislike for negative preaching and writing. It is not sufficient for a speaker or author to discuss the disease, but to satisfy my soul and mind, he must give me the cure. It is easy to point out what is wrong, but I want to know what is right. Sometimes that is a little more difficult than one would suppose. However, when at last honest mistakes have been rectified, and we are back on the paths of truth, it may be that in the providence of God the wrong trail will have left us a heritage of blessing.

---

1.   Charles Price, Chapter IV, *The Real Faith* (Plainfield, New Jersey: Logos International, 1940, 1972). Reprinted by permission of Bridge-Logos.

Many years ago I was on one of my periodic visits to the mountain ranges which border on the rocky coasts of Alaska. A visitor to this land of the Great White Silence had been lost, and I had told him of the trail which would take him back to a valley where he could get his bearings. After a lapse of two hours he was back at my camp. He told me he was confused and completely turned around; and asked me if I would kindly travel with him until he was sure of his direction. I did, for it is a dangerous place in which to wander alone, unless one has a knowledge of the country and its trails. Weeks later I received a letter from the grateful fellow, in which he said among other things, "To know you are on the right trail is a fine thing; but to return to it, after being on the wrong one, multiplies its blessing."

How true! It is after the rain that we appreciate the bursting buds and delicate greens of the early spring. After the storm clouds we appreciate the calm of a sky-blue day. If through these pages I can lead those dear children of God, who have not seen the full fruit of the victory of faith, back to the clear teaching of the Book and to ultimate victory, then this heart of mine will be happy and these pages, written in prayer, will not fail in their mission.

The thing above all else I want you to see is that you can not generate it; you can not work it up; you can not manufacture it. It is imparted and infused by God Himself. You can not sit in your homes and struggle to have faith, and affirm that something *is*; nor can you turn your hope and desire into faith by your own power. The only place you can get it is from the Lord, for the Word clearly and distinctly states that faith is one of two things. It is either a gift of God, or it is a fruit of the Spirit.

We are told in Paul's Epistle to the Corinthians, "Now abideth faith, hope, and love; but the greatest of these is love." While love might be the greatest, it certainly is not the first. It must be proceeded by faith. Look out of your window at yonder tree. What a thing of symmetry and loveliness it is! Only God can make a tree. There is beauty in its twisted branches. There is loveliness in its trembling leaves. Every leaf is a little world unto itself, with its tiny veins carrying the life that God supplies, which gives it all it possesses in its native realm. Yet there is something back of the tree. Beneath the surface of the ground there is a great system of roots hidden away. You never behold them; yet without them the tree would die. It would have no life at all.

FAITH IS THE LIFE

The roots are ugly and hard in comparison to the beautiful greenery about the ground. Yet the greenery is there partly because of those roots. Now, let us call the top of the tree "Love." You can see it. You can contact it. You can enjoy its fragrance. You behold its beauty. It is there because of something which is back of it—something hidden away that causes it. That something is the roots. Now you expect me to say that those roots are the roots of faith. No! *Faith is the life that flows into the roots*. It is that mystical quality that only God can produce and give. There are roots you could plant which never, never grow.

You, yourself, and your inner nature are those roots. Your senses, your avenues of approach to expressions of life itself are buried below the surface where people cannot see them. All the world beholds is what you produce and not you yourself. What did Jesus mean when He said, "By their fruit ye shall know them?" Ye shall know *them*. The fruit produced is an index to what the tree really is.

Let me repeat. The roots of the tree are not faith. The roots do not produce the life, but the life produces the roots. *It is the life that is faith*. It is that wonderful and glorious quality which is a gift of the divine heart, and which sustains us. This life, or faith, will be manifest to the world by the fruit we bear; by the arms of love outstretched; by the things of grace and beauty which through God are manifested day by day on the tree of our lives.

How foolish it would be for that tree to struggle in an attempt to create the life which flows into it. It need not struggle. All it needs to do is to function in obedience to the laws divine. As the life is there, it simply manifests that life in the fruit it bears, and the beauty with which it endows the world.

So it is with faith. Love may be the greatest thing in the world, but faith must of necessity be the first. Without faith it is impossible to please God. But you tell me that *you* have faith. I ask you where you got it. I pick a rosy apple from a tree. I hear it testify from the core of its little apple heart. It tells me it has rosy cheeks. It whispers in my ear that it is so very good to the taste. It invites me to taste its flavor. It testifies that it has so many noble and beautiful qualities. Then I ask it where it got them all.

From the branch? The shelter of the leaves, the rain and the sun? Yes, all true; but I knew that way down in the hidden system, which you can not see, the roots were receiving something from God that no tree on the face of the earth has ever been able to produce of itself!

THE ATHEIST AND GOD

Some time ago an atheist sat in a meeting I was conducting. He was extremely hard and cynical. He lived alone in the room of a hotel, and his solitude had only added to his hard, critical, unbelieving nature. I preached that night on the subject "Comprehending the Incomprehensible." I declared that it was possible to believe the unbelievable; to know the love of God that passeth knowledge. The following morning he came to my room and asked for an interview. He was rather argumentative and I told him, while I did not have time for argument, I would be glad to answer any sincere, honest question which he might put before me.

He said, "I have no faith whatever. I do not believe the Bible, and I do not know if there be a God. I do see a law of order in nature and the universe, but what causes it, or where it came from, I do not know. Now, Dr. Price, your sermon last night was a challenge to my thinking. What I want to know is this: How can a man spend a dollar when he does not have one? How can you drive a car when you do not possess one? How can you believe when you have no belief? How can God expect a man to exercise faith when he does not have any (assuming there is a God)? Where is there any justice in a set-up like that?"

"Are you an honest man, and do you want to know the truth?"

"What is truth?" was the reply. "What brand of it do you mean? I have never been able to find it, although I have spent a lifetime in search of it."

On the wall of my apartment was hanging a picture of Jesus in the Garden of Gethsemane. His hands were clasped and His eyes were raised toward heaven in prayer. I walked over to that picture and looked at it for a moment or two without speaking. I intuitively knew he would be looking at that picture too. When at last I turned to face him, I said, "He is Truth. He is the Way. He is your Life and Faith. He has in abundance what you say you do not have. You have been trying to get it out of mind, thought, and intellect. He can put it there, as the river of His grace flows through your heart. That is why He came. He came to make men free...free from doubts like yours...free from fears and misgivings...free from unbelief and free from sin..."

"Sounds like a fairy story to me," he interrupted. "Fine if you can believe it, but how can man or God expect a man to believe what he can not believe?"

He went away. A week later he came to me and offered his hand. When I looked at his face, I knew the miracle had happened. Into his heart there had come not only the conscious knowledge of sins forgiven, but a manifestation of the sweetness and love of God which had made him a new creation in Christ Jesus. As in the Millennium, instead of the briar shall come up the myrtle tree, so in this man's life there had sprung up the evidence of the Indwelling Presence of God.

"Do you know what happened?" he said. "I told the Lord to manifest Himself, *if He was there*. I asked Him to do something which would reveal His presence, *if He was there at all*. I became conscious that He was near me. I realized *there was a God*—that there was a soul to save. I did not understand it with my mind, but I knew it in my heart. Then I told Him I had no faith to believe, *so He gave me His faith*, and I believed. The work was done."

Why not? That is God's way of salvation. "As many as received Him, to them gave He power to become the Sons of God, even to them that believe on His name." When I give an altar call, I invite *every* man, and *every* woman, to surrender his heart and life to Christ. If we are saved by Faith, how do I know that all can have the faith to receive? How did I know that *every one* whom I invite can find eternal life? Some might have faith, and others be entirely devoid of it. The fact that people *believe what you say* does not mean that they have the faith to translate that belief, or even heart hunger, into an experimental knowledge of sins forgiven.

Nevertheless, I cry "Whosoever will may come," because I know that He will *impart the faith which is needful* to every sincere heart. I have quoted the twelfth verse of the first chapter of John: "But as many as received Him, to them gave He power to become the Sons of God, even to them that believe on His name." Let me quote the next one. Thus does it read: "Who were born (that is, born again) not of blood, nor of the *will of flesh, nor of the will of man,* but of God."

The same Holy Ghost who convicts the sinner of his sin will see to it that as the sinner was given enough conviction to convince him of his sin, so he will now be given faith enough to convince him of his salvation. But no man *in himself* possesses that faith. Are we not told "By grace are ye saved, through *faith;* and *that not of yourselves; it is the gift of God.*" Poor, wretched, miserable, ignorant, unbelieving humanity could never grow or develop in such corrupt hearts of unbelief faith enough to believe in a Saviour, let alone receive Him. So the Holy Spirit not only imparts the conviction of the need of a Saviour, but also imparts the faith to receive Him.

Never think it was *your* faith that received Christ as your Saviour. Never say that any act of yours was the basis of your redemption. It is Jesus who imparts the water of which He spoke to the woman by Samaria's wayside well. It is Jesus who puts His arms of love beneath the burden on your back and lifts it from your tired, weary body. It is Jesus who pours into the lacerated, broken heart the oil of heaven's joy. It is Jesus who smoothes the wrinkles of care with the gentle touch of a mother's hand, and it is Jesus who brings you out of the darkness of the night into the light of His own glorious and wonderful day.

"Oh, it is Jesus; yes, it is Jesus;
Yes, it is Jesus in my soul;
For I have touched the hem of His garment,
And His blood has made me whole!"

Sing it and shout it. Proclaim it and herald it near and far. His blood—His grace—His power—His pardon—His *faith!*

A LIVING FAITH

When will we stop our foolish and needless struggles and begin to believe? When will we put an end to our unscriptural mental and intellectual gyrations in our attempt to find a faith we do not possess; for unless we get it from God, never will we possess that Faith! We are capable of belief and at the same time absolutely incapable of the exercise of Bible faith. Thousands have wandered into the error of thinking that belief is faith. *It is not.* There is belief in faith, without a doubt; but *"the devils also believe."* Belief is cold—intellectual. It operates as far as the human goes in the realms of intellect. Many sinful men *believe the Bible*, but *such belief does not save them.*

Faith is living. It moves and operates, and sweeps the enemies of the soul before its irresistible march. All the faith in the world? No! You need only as much as a grain of mustard seed, if it is God's faith! Then mountains will be removed. Your sin-sick soul will behold the glory of the Lord. But it must be God's faith. It must come from Him. He must impart it. And *He will*. That is the Gospel of Grace which I believe.

The Jericho Road *without* Jesus is the Jericho Road. *With Him* it is the shining highway of salvation and healing. Its very rocks cry out His glory. *Without Him* its dust is sordid, its tears are real, and its blindness is so dark; but *with Him* its dust begins to grow the flowers of grace and glory; its tears are turned to pearls; its blindness and darkness is turned to light. It takes the presence of Jesus to work the miracle of the transformation of the Jericho Road.

The blind man did not sit in the sand and say to himself, "I am healed—I can see—I can see—now if only I can *believe* I am healed and can see, then I will be!..." No. He heard that Jesus of Nazareth was passing by. He cried, "Jesus! Jesus! Help me! Please help me, for I can not help myself!" Then do not forget the words of Jesus, *"What wilt thou that I should do unto thee?"* Mark you, it was not *"What wilt thou that you should do,"* but *"What do you want Me to do?"*

True, He said, "Go thy way; thy faith hath made thee whole." "Thy faith," said Jesus. Where did the blind man get it? Who gave it to him? If it was his faith all the time, why was he not healed before Jesus came that way? If you give me a watch, it is my watch. But I got it from you. There is faith in my heart as I write, but I know where I got it. Not affirmation—not from will—not from belief—not from mental grasps or understanding—but from Jesus. He is the Author and Finisher of *our* faith. Oh, matchless grace! Oh, love divine, all love excelling! Thus has the joy of heaven to earth come down!

Once upon a time there was a tiny little seed planted in the ground. It was an acorn. After a while it shed its little overcoat and cuddled away in the arms of mother nature, so that it might be fed and grow. All through the long winter night she kept that little seed warm; and when the springtime sun came out, its little acorn heart burst open with joy and delight. It started to grow. Then a man came along and put a big heavy rock over the little seed. It commenced to worry and to fret for fear it would never be able to raise its little head to where it could see the light of day. It wanted to wear a garland of leaves for its hair, and to grow to be beautiful and strong.

One day its feeble hands touched the rock. They were such tiny, tender little hands. The little growing tree felt so helpless. It did not struggle or try to move the rock which was the enemy of its heart and life. It just grew. One day the rock was lifted. It was pushed out of the way; and the little leafy hands clapped for joy. Who lifted the rock? The seed? No! It was something within the seed which no man in the world has ever been able to reproduce. It was God's power that pushed over that rock.

My friend, you are a little seed. You, too, can grow into something noble and beautiful for God. The power of faith can be manifested in your life until men and angels will wonder. However, when the battle is over and the victory has been won, do not say, "Look at what I have done through the Lord," but rather kneel at the foot of the cross and say, "Is it not wonderful that His grace and His faith should be manifested in me!"

Chapter 5

Part I

The Passion for the Alongside One

FATHER GOD WE KNOW, Jesus Christ we know, but who is the Holy Spirit?

Much of the Church lives as though the Spirit does not exist. We have a theology of the Spirit, but we have little significant consciousness of His Presence and little dynamic testimony of His power. All our symbolic terms for the Holy Spirit (wind, fire, dove, etc.) only add to our confusion by depersonalizing His dynamic nature in the Godhead and depreciating His profound involvement with mankind.

It is very clear that the Old Testament writers understood the reality of the Spirit's personality and the necessity of His interactions with the human race.

> But Moses said to him, "Are you jealous for my sake? Would that all the Lord's people were prophets, that the Lord would put His Spirit upon them!" (Numbers 11:29)

> And I will put My Spirit within you and cause you to walk in My statutes, and you will be careful to observe My ordinances (Ezekiel 36:27).

And it will come about after this that I will pour out My Spirit on all mankind; and your sons and daughters will prophesy, your old men will dream dreams, your young men will see visions (Joel 2:28).

The contemplative writers of the past recognized the significance of the Spirit's place in the determinations of God as well as His irreplaceable importance in the eternal operations of the Father.

> "It is certain from the Holy Scriptures (Rom. viii.; John xiv.,) that the Spirit of God dwells within us, acts there, prays without ceasing, groans, desires, asks for us what we know not how to ask for ourselves, urges us on, animates us, speaks to us when we are silent, suggests to us all truth, and so unites us to Him that we become one spirit. (1 Cor. vi. 17.)"[1]

Thomas Arnold said, "It is the very main thing of all. We are living under the dispensation of the spirit; in that character God now reveals Himself to His people. He who knows not God the Holy Ghost cannot know God at all."[2]

Samuel Chadwick emphasized the Spirit's role with these words: "The Holy Scriptures declare Him to be the Revealer of all truth, the active agent in all works of redemption, and from first to last the instrument of Grace in the experience of salvation. Illumination and Conviction, Repentance and Regeneration, Assurance and Sanctification, are all work of God the eternal Spirit."[3]

Listen to the words of the early Church fathers as they described their conviction concerning the Holy Spirit in the Nicene Creed:

> "And I believe in the Holy Ghost the Lord, and Giver of Life,
> who proceedeth from the Father [and the Son];
> who with the Father and the Son together
> is worshipped and glorified...."[4]

---

1. François Fénelon, *Spiritual Progress*, James W. Metcalf, ed. (New York: M.W. Dodd, 1853). March 25, 1997. October 7, 1999. <http://www.ccel.org/f/fenelon/progress/spirit02.htm/>.

2. Samuel Chadwick, *The Way to Pentecost* (Dixon, Missouri: Rare Christian Books), 9.

3. Chadwick, *The Way to Pentecost*, 9.

4. The Nicene Creed. October 2, 1999. October 7, 1999. <http://www.forerunner.com/chalcedon/X009 4. Nicene Creed.html/>.

The Holy Spirit is the ultimate contributor of revelation and the unique enforcer of redemption. He proceeds from the Father as the active agent for the purposes of God in the earth. He is the interior expression of the unseen God's personality as well as the visible manifestation of His activity in the world. Through the Spirit we are able to enjoy intimacy with the awesome God of the universe. God's ultimate desire to live with His people is made possible through the Holy Spirit.

The Spirit is not matter; neither is He material. He does not have substance, size, or weight. He does not take up space; the Spirit can occupy the same space as matter. In fact, the Spirit needs a body through which to express Himself. Hebrews 10:5 says that God prepared a body for the Lord Jesus. Matthew 1 says that the body of the Lord Jesus was conceived by the Holy Spirit. The Holy Spirit prepared a body for the Lord to inhabit so that the mighty will and work of God could be manifested in the earth. The finished work of the Lord Jesus then formed the "body of Christ" so that the same Spirit might indwell the believer and express the will and work of God in the earth.

It is through our bodies that the Spirit is able to accomplish God's purposes in the world. As we submit to Him, He is able to *touch* mankind. The union of the Spirit and the submissive will of man creates an opportunity for God to communicate with His creation.

Resistance to His interior promptings results in an internal *grieving* on the part of the Spirit. Our willful pride and insistence on our own selfish way hinders the Spirit's ability to change us into vessels worthy and able to impact the world for the Kingdom. This hindrance pains the Spirit and interrupts the progression of God's eternal plan in the universe.

The relation of Jesus to the Holy Spirit.

The Holy Spirit was the conceiving power in the birth of Jesus. As the Divine Tutor He jealously watched over the growth and development of the Son of God in human form. When the Spirit of God descended upon Jesus at His baptism, He became the empowering Presence and the interior energy throughout the Son's life. After the baptism by John, the Spirit led Jesus into the wilderness for His first recorded victorious confrontation with Beelzebub. He came out of that wilderness strengthened by the Spirit. By the power of the Spirit, Jesus cast out demons, healed the sick, and delivered the oppressed.

But when he had considered this, behold, an angel of the Lord appeared to him in a dream, saying, "Joseph, son of David, do not be afraid to take Mary as your wife; for that which has been conceived in her is of the Holy Spirit" (Matthew 1:20).

And after being baptized, Jesus went up immediately from the water; and behold, the heavens were opened, and he saw the Spirit of God descending as a dove, and coming upon Him (Matthew 3:16).

Then Jesus was led up by the Spirit into the wilderness to be tempted by the devil (Matthew 4:1).

Behold, My Servant whom I have chosen; My Beloved in whom My soul is well-pleased; I will put My Spirit upon Him, and He shall proclaim justice to the Gentiles (Matthew 12:18).

But if I cast out demons by the Spirit of God, then the kingdom of God has come upon you (Matthew 12:28).

The Spirit of the Lord is upon Me, because He anointed Me to preach the gospel to the poor. He has sent Me to proclaim release to the captives, and recovery of sight to the blind, to set free those who are downtrodden (Luke 4:18).

This dynamic relationship between the Holy Spirit and Jesus continued throughout His life. Jesus passionately relied upon the vitality that was produced by His intense immersion into the Spirit's enabling power.

The Spirit is the Empowering Presence.

Jesus' most passionate words concerning the Holy Spirit were spoken at the last meal He shared with His loved ones, while the horrors of His death loomed over Him. His disciples were struggling with the bewildering implications of His announced soon departure. A sense of dread fell over the room as their beloved Master spoke of His impending death. The disciples could not imagine the pain of being left *alone*. For three years they had lived and breathed in His all-comforting Presence, and they had grown so much in grace. But they also were painfully aware of how much more they had to learn. They had thought that they would have many years with Him! They were not ready for Him to go. Surely He was mistaken. He had so much more good to do, so many more lives to touch. This just could not be happening.

Jesus, knowing their bewilderment and fear, attempted to comfort them with these words: "And I will ask the Father, and He will give you another Helper, that He may be with you forever."[5]

In the light of His soon-coming death, resurrection, and ascension, Jesus petitioned the Father to send help to His struggling disciples. The answer? Another Helper. A look at these two words in the Greek will help us to more accurately understand His prayer. The Greek word for "Helper" is *paraklesis*. It is a combination of two root words: *para*, "besides," and *klesis*, "to call." The combined meaning is "the called alongside one."[6]

There are two Greek words for "other": *allos* and *heteros*. *Heteros* means "another of a different kind," while *allos* means "another of the same kind."[7] Jesus used the word *allos*. He was telling His disciples that He was going to send another Helper who would be to them all that He had been. As He had been a source of life and grace to them, so too the Spirit would be.

Combining the two thoughts, Jesus promised that He would send One exactly like Himself to be with them at all times. *Jesus clearly understood the vital connection between the intimacy with the Holy Spirit and the continuance of His ministry on the earth through the disciples.*

The disciples had already felt the presence of the Spirit *with* them, but now He was coming to abide *in* them. He would be the fountainhead of their growth and the dynamism for their ministry. He came as the empowering Presence of God that would be with them at all times—forever. It was comparable to having Jesus personally with them every moment of every day for the rest of their lives. At the time the disciples could not understand the import of that statement, but they soon personally experienced the power of the indwelling Spirit of God, and it forever changed them.

"If the church is going to be effective in the post modern world, we need to stop paying lip service to the Spirit and to recapture Paul's perspective: the Spirit as the *experienced, empowering* return

---

5.   John 14:16.

6.   W.E. Vine, Merrill F. Unger, and William White, Jr., *Vine's Complete Expository Dictionary of Old and New Testament Words* (Nashville, Tennessee: Thomas Nelson, 1985), 110-111.

7.   W.E. Vine, Merrill F. Unger, and William White, Jr., *Vine's Complete Expository Dictionary of Old and New Testament Words* (Nashville, Tennessee: Thomas Nelson, 1985), 451.

of God's own *personal presence* in and among us, who enables us to live as a radically *eschatological* people in the present world while we await the consummation....

"The result is that by the Spirit's coming, the veil is removed, both from our faces and from the Presence, so that we can behold the glory of the Lord himself in the face of God's Son, our Lord Jesus Christ. By the Spirit's presence one is now behind the veil in the very presence of God, not only beholding God's glory in Christ but also being transformed into God's likeness from one degree of glory to another."[8]

The Holy Spirit is the Representative Emissary of Jesus.

When the Helper comes, whom I will send to you from the Father, that is the Spirit of truth, who proceeds from the Father, He will bear witness of Me (John 15:26).

As the Holy Spirit was the enabling power in the life of Jesus, so now He is the testimonial witness *for* Jesus. He will call no attention to Himself but will point all men to the irresistible Son. Through the influence of internal inspiration, the Spirit will impart to men understanding of the Person and purposes of the Lord Jesus. He will search out all truth and bring its illuminating force to bear upon the spirit of man.

The Holy Spirit does not have His own personal agenda. The works of Jesus is His agenda. The same intimacy of relationship and passion of purpose that existed between Jesus and the Holy Spirit will be perpetuated by the Spirit's interaction with all future disciples of the Lord Jesus.

When Jesus spoke of the disciples doing "greater works," He was declaring that the Holy Spirit would carry on the work that the Son had begun through each one of His disciples. The "greater works" that Jesus prophesied of would find reality through the internal dynamic of the Spirit of God in the lives of the disciples, exponentially multiplying the work that the Son had begun.[9]

---

8.   Gordon Fee, *Paul, the Spirit, and the People of God* (Peabody, Massachusetts: Hendrickson Publishers, 1996), xv, 21.

9.   See John 14:12.

The Spirit will always direct the focus of God's people toward the Lord Jesus...in their worship, their meditations, their life experiences, and their work. All culminates in the Son of the Father's love.

"An advocate appears as representative of another, and the Holy Spirit appears as representative of another, and the Holy Spirit comes to represent Christ, interpret and vindicate Christ, administer for Christ in His Church and Kingdom; to be to the believer all that Christ Himself was, and is—with this difference, that the Christ was with His disciples and the Spirit is in them."[10]

The Holy Spirit is the believer's Divine Director.

The mystics of centuries past believed strongly in the importance of having a spiritual director. This spiritually mature person acted as an assistant in their search for ultimate truth and reality, elucidating on the path that leads to union with God.

The Holy Spirit is our Divine Director. He is the One who leads us to the enlightenment of spiritual absolutes and the experience of hidden realities. He is the "Speaker of the House." There is no other who can better represent to the believer the will and heart of God. He takes the mysteries of the spiritual Kingdom and illumines our hearts so we can perceive the true spiritual nature of the world in which we live.

But the Helper, the Holy Spirit, whom the Father will send in My name, He will teach you all things, and bring to your remembrance all that I said to you (John 14:26).

Too often the Church has rejected the revelatory assistance of the Holy Spirit. We have turned, again and again, to the false foundation of the natural mind. We have attempted to uncover the veritable realities of spiritual things through human knowledge. Our schools of learning have produced learned men and women who understand biblical languages, textual criticisms, theological truths, and historical continuities. As the Body of Christ, we have feasted from the tree of the knowledge of good and evil, but it has not advanced our spiritual perception and power.

We do not advance toward God through the mind. It is only by the Spirit that we can know and experience God. The Holy Spirit is the only

---

10.   Samuel Chadwick, *The Way to Pentecost*, 23.

divinely approved Guide in the realm of spiritual pursuits. Let's read from Fénelon again:

> "It is certain from the Holy Scriptures (Rom. viii.; John xiv.,) that the Spirit of God dwells within us, acts there, prays without ceasing, groans, desires, asks for us what we know not how to ask for ourselves, urges us on, animates us, speaks to us when we are silent, suggests to us all truth, and so unites us to Him that we become one spirit. (1 Cor. vi. 17.) This is the teaching of faith, and even those instructors who are farthest removed from the interior life, cannot avoid acknowledging so much. Still, notwithstanding these theoretical principles, they always strive to maintain that in practice the external law, or at least a certain light of learning and reason, illuminates us within, and that then our understanding acts of itself from that instruction. They do not rely sufficiently upon the interior teacher, the Holy Spirit, who does everything in us. He is the soul of our soul; we could not form a thought or a desire without Him. Alas! what blindness is ours! We reckon ourselves alone in the interior sanctuary, when God is much more intimately present there than we are ourselves."[11]

The Holy Spirit is the Dynamic of God.

And Jesus returned to Galilee in the power of the Spirit; and news about Him spread through all the surrounding district (Luke 4:14).

The Holy Spirit is the creative expression of the power of God. Every manifestation of the power of God in this world is accomplished through the agency of the Holy Spirit. There are no boundaries to the Spirit's ability to express Himself in life. There is no sickness that cannot be cured. There is no insurmountable task that cannot be accomplished; nor is there any human situation that cannot be corrected by the dynamic influence of the Holy Spirit.

Led by the Spirit, Jesus searched for those casualties of life who were waiting and willing to be exposed to the "enabling influence" of the Spirit of God, who was resident in fullness in the Lord Jesus.

---

11. Fénelon, *Spiritual Progress.* March 25, 1997. October 7, 1999. <http://www.ccel.org/f/fenelon/progress/spirit02.htm/>.

The cessation of miracles and power-manifestations of the Holy Spirit is not the result of a dispensational time clock. They did not disappear because we now have the Bible for our guidance and spiritual maturation.

Their absence from the life of the average believer is the direct result of men's forsaking the internal operation of the Holy Spirit. This seeming suspension of the Holy Spirit's activity in the earth is the natural consequence of the Church's lack of commitment to and reliance upon this holy member of the Godhead.

The return of the Holy Spirit to prominence in the lives of God's people will lead to a resurrection of the miraculous. First, though, we must overcome the years of staunch unbelief in our hearts and of our prideful confidence in our abilities. As faith arises and self is laid low, the possibilities in the Spirit grow beyond anything we could even begin to imagine.

As the Son walked in the dynamic of the Spirit, so now He prepares His future disciples to receive that power into their lives.

And when He had said this, He breathed on them, and said to them, "Receive the Holy Spirit" (John 20:22).

Receive the Holy Spirit!

Chapter 5

Part II

At the Master's Feet[1]

Sadhu Sundar Singh was born in an aristocratic Sikh family in Rampur, India. He aggressively sought God in Sikhism, Hinduism, Buddhism, and Islam. At the age of 15, in great disillusionment, he decided to take his life. He planned to lie down on a train track and see if, through death, he might find God on the other side.

At 3 o'clock on the morning of the day he had planned to end his life, a miracle happened. A great light appeared in his room and he heard in perfect Hindustani these words: "Why do you persecute Me? Remember that I gave My life for you upon the cross." He immediately fell to his knees and worshiped Jesus.

Sadhu committed the rest of his life in service to this same Jesus. During the course of his life the Lord would speak to him many times through visual encounters. At the Master's Feet is an account of some of those divine encounters.

Throughout this writing Sadhu refers to the transforming power of the Holy Spirit. He also refers to his own inabilities when he was without that dynamic in his life, which is emphasized in his prayer, "My Lord God, my all

---

1.   Sadhu Sundar Singh, *At the Master's Feet*, Rev. Arthur and Mrs. Parker, trans. (London and Edinburgh: Fleming H. Revell Company, 1922). June 25, 1997. October 5, 1999.

in all, life of my life, and spirit of my spirit, look in mercy upon me and so fill me with Thy Holy Spirit that my heart shall have no room for love of aught but Thee."

* * *

Sadhu Sundar Singh

INTRODUCTION

First Vision

Once on a dark night I went alone into the forest to pray, and seating myself upon a rock I laid before God my deep necessities, and besought His help. After a short time, seeing a poor man coming towards me I thought he had come to ask me for some relief because he was hungry and cold. I said to him, "I am a poor man, and except this blanket I have nothing at all. You had better go to the village near by and ask for help there." And lo! even whilst I was saying this he flashed forth like lightning, and, showering drops of blessing, immediately disappeared. Alas! Alas! it was now clear to me that this was my beloved Master who came not to beg from a poor creature like me, but to bless and to enrich me (2 Cor. viii.9), and so I was left weeping and lamenting my folly and lack of insight.

Second Vision

On another day, my work being finished, I again went into the forest to pray, and seated upon that same rock began to consider for what blessings I should make petition. Whilst thus engaged it seemed to me that another came and stood near me, who, judged by his bearing and dress and manner of speech, appeared to be a revered and devoted servant of God; but his eyes glittered with craft and cunning, and as he spoke he seemed to breathe an odour of hell.

He thus addressed me, "Holy and Honoured Sir, pardon me for interrupting your prayers and breaking in on your privacy; but is one's duty to seek to promote the advantage of others, and therefore I have come to lay an important matter before you. Your pure and unselfish life has made a deep impression not only on me, but upon a great number of devout persons. But although in the Name of God you have sacrificed yourself body and soul for others, you have never been truly appreciated. My meaning is that being a Christian only a few thousand Christians have come under your influence, and some even of these distrust you. How much better would it be if you became a Hindu or a

Mussulman, and thus become a great leader indeed? They are in search of such a spiritual head. If you accept this suggestion of mine, then three hundred and ten millions of Hindus and Mussulmans will become your followers, and render you reverent homage."

As soon as I heard this there rushed from my lips these words, "Thou Satan! get thee hence. I knew at once that thou wert a wolf in sheep's clothing! Thy one wish is that I should give up the cross and the narrow path that leads to life, and choose the broad road of death. My Master Himself is my lot and my portion, who Himself gave His life for me, and it behooves me to offer as a sacrifice my life and all I have to Him who is all in all to me. Get you gone therefore, for with you I have nothing to do."

Hearing this he went off grumbling and growling in his rage. And I, in tears, thus poured out my soul to God in prayer, "My Lord God, my all in all, life of my life, and spirit of my spirit, look in mercy upon me and so fill me with Thy Holy Spirit that my heart shall have no room for love of aught but Thee. I seek from Thee no other gift but Thyself, who art the Giver of life and all its blessings. From Thee I ask not for the world or its treasures, nor yet for heaven even make request, but Thee alone do I desire and long for, and where Thou art there is Heaven. The hunger and the thirst of this heart of mine can be satisfied only with Thee who hast given it birth. O Creator mine! Thou hast created my heart for Thyself alone, and not for another, therefore this my heart can find no rest or ease save in Thee, in Thee who hast both created it and set in it this very longing for rest. Take away then from my heart all that is opposed to Thee, and enter and abide and rule for ever. Amen."

When I rose up from this prayer I beheld a glowing Being, arrayed in light and beauty, standing before me. Though He spoke not a word, and because my eyes were suffused with tears I saw Him not too clearly, there poured from Him lightning-like rays of life-giving love with such power that they entered in and bathed my very soul. At once I knew that my dear Saviour stood before me. I rose at once from the rock where I was seated and fell at His feet. He held in His hand the key of my heart. Opening the inner chamber of my heart with His key of love, He filled it with His presence, and wherever I looked, inside or out, I saw but Him.

Then did I know that man's heart is the very throne and citadel of God, and that when He enters there to abide, heaven begins. In these few seconds He so filled my heart, and spoke such wonderful words, that even if I wrote many books I could not tell them all. For these heavenly things can be explained only in heavenly language, and earthly tongues are not sufficient for them. Yet I will endeavour to set down a few of these heavenly things that by way of vision came to me from the Master. Upon the rock on which before I sat He seated Himself, and with myself at His feet there began between Master and disciple the conversation that now follows.

SECTION I

The Disciple,—O Master, Fountain of life! Why dost Thou hide Thyself from those that adore Thee, and dost not rejoice the eyes of them that long to gaze upon Thee?

The Master,—1. My true child, true happiness depends not upon the sight of the eyes, but comes through spiritual vision, and depends upon the heart. In Palestine thousands looked upon Me, but all of them did not thus obtain true happiness. By mortal eyes only those things can be perceived that are mortal, for eyes of flesh cannot behold an immortal God and spiritual beings. For instance, you yourself cannot see your own spirit, therefore how can you behold its Creator? But when the spiritual eyes are opened, then you can surely see Him who is Spirit, (John iv.24), and that which you now see of Me you see not with eyes of flesh, but with the eyes of the spirit.

If, as you say, thousands of people saw Me in Palestine then were all their spiritual eyes opened, or did I Myself become mortal? The answer is, No! I took on a mortal body so that in it I might give a ransom for the sins of the world; and when the work of salvation was completed for sinners (John xix.30), then that which was immortal transfigured what was mortal into glory. Therefore after the resurrection only those were able to see Me who had received spiritual sight (Acts x. 40,41).

2. Many there are in this world who know about Me, but do not know Me; that is they have no personal relationship with Me, therefore they have no true apprehension of or faith in Me, and do not accept Me as their Saviour and Lord.

Just as if one talks with a man born blind about different colors such as red, blue, yellow, he remains absolutely unaware of their charm and beauty, he cannot attach any value to them, because he only knows about them, and is aware of their various names. But with regard to colors he can have no true conception until his eyes are opened. In the same manner until a man's spiritual eyes are opened, howsoever learned he may be, he cannot know Me, he cannot behold My glory, and he cannot understand that I am God Incarnate.

3. There are many believers who are aware of My presence in their hearts bringing to them spiritual life and peace, but cannot plainly see Me. Just as the

eye can see many things, yet when someone drops medicine into the eye does not see it, but the presence of the medicine is felt cleansing the inner eye and promoting the power of sight.

4. The true peace which is born of My presence in the hearts of true believers they are unable to see, but, feeling its power, they become happy in it. Nor can they see that happiness of mind or heart through which they enjoy the peace of My presence. It is the same with the tongue and sweetmeats. The faculty of taste which resides in the tongue and the sweetness it perceives are both invisible. Thus also I give My children life and joy by means of the hidden manna, which the world with all its wisdom knows not nor can know (Rev. ii.7).

5. Sometimes during sickness the faculty of taste in the tongue is interfered with, and during that time, however tasty the food given to the sick person may be, it has an ill taste to him. In just the same way sin interferes with the taste for spiritual things. Under such circumstances My Word and service and My presence lost their attraction to the sinner, and instead of profiting by them he begins to argue about and to criticize them.

6. Many believers again—like the man born blind, on receiving his sight—are able to see Jesus as a prophet and the Son of Man, but do not regard Him as the Christ and the Son of God (John ix.17, 35-37), until I am revealed to them a second time in power.

7. A mother once hid herself in a garden amongst some densely growing shrubs, and her little son went in search of her here and there, crying as he went. Through the whole garden he went, but could not find her. A servant said to him, "Sonny, don't cry! Look at the mangoes on this tree and all the pretty, pretty flowers in the garden. Come, I am going to get some for you." But the child cried out, "No! No! I want my mother. The food she gives me is nicer than all the mangoes, and her love is sweeter far than all these flowers, and indeed you know that all this garden is mine, for all that my mother has is mine. No! I want my mother!" When the mother, hidden in the bushes, heard this, she rushed out and, snatching her child to her breast, smothered him with kisses, and that garden became a paradise to the child. In this way My children cannot find in this great garden of a world, so full of charming and beautiful things, any true joy until they find Me. I am their Emmanuel, who is ever with them, and I make Myself known to them (John xiv.21).

8. Just as the sponge lies in the water, and the water fills the sponge, but the water is not the sponge and the sponge is not the water, but they ever remain different things, so children abide in Me and I in them. This is not pantheism, but it is the kingdom of God, which is set up in the hearts of those who abide

in this world; and just as the water in the sponge, I am in every place and in everything, but they are not I (Luke xvii.21).

9. Take a piece of charcoal, and however much you may wash it its blackness will not disappear, but let the fire enter into it and its dark colour vanishes. So also when the sinner receives the Holy Spirit (who is from the Father and Myself, for the Father and I are one), which is the baptism of fire, all the blackness of sin is driven away, and he is made a light to the world (Matt. iii.11, v.14). As the fire in the charcoal, so I abide in My children and they in Me, and through them I make Myself manifest to the world.

SECTION II

The Disciple,—Master, if Thou wouldst make a special manifestation of Thyself to the world, men would no longer doubt the existence of God and Thy own divinity, but all would believe and enter on the path of righteousness.

The Master,—1. My son, the inner state of every man I know well, and to each heart in accordance with its needs I make Myself known; and for bringing men into the way of righteousness there is no better means than the manifestation of Myself. For man I became man that he might know God, not as someone terrible and foreign, but as full of love and like to himself, for he is like Him and made in His image.

Man also has a natural desire that he should see Him in whom he believes and who loves him. But the Father cannot be seen, for He is by nature incomprehensible, and he who would comprehend Him must have the same nature. But man is a comprehensible creature, and being so cannot see God. Since, however, God is Love and He has given to man that same faculty of love, therefore, in order that that craving for love might be satisfied, He adopted a form of existence that man could comprehend. Thus He became man, and His children with all the holy angels may see Him and enjoy Him (Col. i.15, ii.9). Therefore I said that he that hath seen Me hath seen the Father (John xiv.9-10). And although while in the form of man I am called the Son, I am the eternal and everlasting Father (Isa. ix.6).

2. I and the Father and the Holy Spirit are One. Just as in the sun there are both heat and light, but the light is not heat, and the heat is not light, but both are one, though in their manifestation they have different forms, so I and the Holy Spirit, proceeding from the Father, bring light and heat to the world. The Spirit, which is the baptismal fire, burns to ashes in the hearts of believers all manner of sin and iniquity, making them pure and holy. I who am the True Light

(John i.9, viii.12), dissipate all dark and evil desires, and leading them in the way of righteousness bring them at last to their eternal home. Yet We are not three but One, just as the sun is but one.

3. Whatever worth and power and high faculty God has endowed man with must be brought into action, otherwise they gradually decay and die. In this way faith, if it is not truly fixed on the living God, is shattered by the shock of sin and transformed into doubt. Often one hears something like this, "If this or that doubt of mine be removed I am ready to believe." That is as though one with a broken limb should ask the doctor to take away the pain before he sets the limb. Surely this is folly, for the pain comes from the breaking of the limb, and when that is set the pain will of itself pass away. Thus by the act of sin man's tie with God has been snapped, and doubts, which are spiritual pains, have arisen. It needs must, therefore, that the union with God be again renewed, then those doubts which have arisen regarding My divinity and the existence of God will of themselves disappear. Then in place of pain there will come that wonderful peace which the world cannot give nor take away. Thus it was that I became flesh, that between God and poor broken men there might be union, and they might be happy with Him in heaven for evermore.

4. God is love, and in every living creature He has set this faculty of love, but especially in man. It is therefore nothing but right that the Lover who has given us life and reason and love itself should receive His due tribute of love. His desire is to all He has created, and if this love be not rightly used, and if we do not with all our heart and soul and mind and strength love Him who has endowed us with love, then that love falls from its high estate and becomes selfishness. Thus arises disaster both for ourselves and for other creatures of God. Every selfish man, strangely enough, becomes a self-slayer.

This also I have said, "Love thy neighbour as thyself." Now although in a sense all men are neighbours one of another, yet the reference is especially to those who habitually live near each other, for it is an easy matter to live at peace with one who is near at hand for a few days only, even though he be unfriendly; but in the case of one who has his dwelling near you, and day by day is the cause of trouble to you, it is most difficult to bear with him, and love him as yourself. But when you have conquered in this great struggle it will be more easy to love all others as yourself.

When man with all his heart, mind, and soul loves God, and his neighbour as himself there will be no room for doubts, but in him will be established that Kingdom of God of which there should be no end, and he, melted and moulded in the fire of love, will be made into the image of his heavenly Father, who at the first made him like Himself.

5. Also I manifest Myself by means of My Word (the Bible) to those who seek Me with a sincere heart. Just as for the salvation of men I took on a human body, so My Word also, which is Spirit and Life (John vi.63) is written in the language of men, that is, there are inspired and human elements united in it. But just as men do not understand Me, so they do not understand My Word. To understand it a knowledge of the Hebrew and Greek tongues is not a necessity, but what is necessary is the fellowship of that Holy Spirit, abiding in whom the prophets and apostles wrote it. Without doubt the language of this Word is spiritual, and he who is born of the Spirit is alone able fully to understand it, whether he be acquainted with the criticism of the world or be only a child, for that spiritual language is well understood by him since it is his mother tongue. But remember that those whose wisdom is only of this world cannot understand it, for they have no share in the Holy Spirit.

6. In the book of nature, of which I also am the Author, I freely manifest Myself. But for the reading of this book also spiritual insight is needed, that men may find Me, otherwise there is a danger lest instead of finding Me they go astray.

Thus the blind man uses the tips of his fingers as eyes, and by means of touch alone reads a book, but by touch alone can form no real estimate of its truth. The investigations of agnostics and sceptics prove this, for in place of perfection they see only defects. Fault finding critics ask, "If there is an Almighty Creator of the world why are there defects in it, such as hurricanes, earthquakes, eclipses, pain, suffering, death, and the like?" The folly of this criticism is similar to that of an unlearned man who finds fault with an unfinished building or an incomplete picture. After a time, when he sees them fully finished, he is ashamed of his folly, and ends by singing their praises. Thus too, God did not in one day give to this world its present form, nor will it in one day reach perfection. The whole creation moves onward to perfection, and if it were possible for the man of this world to see from afar with the eyes of God the perfect world in which no defect appears, he too would bow in praise before Him and say, "All is very good" (Gen. i.31).

7. The human spirit abides in the body very much as the chicken in the shell. If it were possible for the bird within the shell to be told that outside of it was a great widespread world, with all kinds of fruit and flowers, with rivers and grand mountains, that its mother also was there, and that it would see all this when set free from its shell, it could not understand or believe it. Even if

anyone told it that its feathers and eyes, ready now for use, would enable it to see and to fly, it would not believe it, nor would any proof be possible till it came out of its shell.

In the same way there are many who are uncertain about the future life and the existence of God, because they cannot see beyond this shell-like body of flesh, and their thoughts, like delicate wings, cannot carry them beyond the narrow confines of the brain. Their weak eyes cannot discover those eternal and unfading treasures which God has prepared for those who love Him (Isa. lxiv.4, lxv.17). The necessary condition for attaining to this eternal life is this, that while still in this body we should receive from the Holy Spirit by faith that life-giving warmth which the chicken receives from its mother, otherwise there is danger of death and eternal loss.

8. Again, many say that the thing, or the life, that has a beginning must of necessity have an end. This is not true, for is not the Almighty who is able at His will to make from naught a thing which is, also able by the word of His power to confer immortality on that which He has made? If not He cannot be called Almighty. Life in this world appears to be liable to decay and destruction, because it is in subjection to those things which are themselves the subject of change and decay. But if this life were set free from these changeful and decaying influences, and brought under the care of the eternal and unchanging God, who is the fountain and source of eternal life, it would escape from the clutch of death and attain to eternity.

As for those who believe on Me, "I give unto them eternal life, and they shall never perish, neither shall any man pluck them out of My hand" (John x.28). "I am the Lord God Almighty that is and was and is to come" (Rev. i.8).

Chapter 6

Part I

The Passion for the Working God

ELOHIM, YAHWEH, EL ELYON, ADONAI, JEHOVAH, EL SHADDAI...these are some of the sacred Hebraic names attributed to the God of Israel. No other Hebrew terms elicited such awe and reverence. The articulation of these names of God inspired the hearer to lofty contemplation of the One who dwells in the obscurity of eternity. Yahweh's infrequent appearances in Israel's history just enhanced the mystery surrounding Him. Enshrouded in transcendent glory, unapproachable by man—very few in the annals of Jewish literature could claim to have met this Most High God. As a result, these mysterious encounters with the Immortal God only served to increase the enigma that cloaked the Almighty.

Who could ascend to the lofty places where God dwells and return with a knowledge of the Most High? If you had indeed encountered Him, how would you describe Him? What words would best communicate His majestic presence and nature to mankind?

In the celebrated Sermon on the Mount, Jesus chose a most unusual word for God. "Let your light shine before men in such a way that they may see your good works, and glorify your Father who is in heaven."[1] Father?

---

1.   Matthew 5:16.

Did He say *Father*? No doubt there was a stir among the crowd as the people asked one another if they had heard correctly. Was this a new word for the fearsome God of their historical accounts? What a strange concept to use for the Almighty, the God who had thundered from Mount Sinai before their ancestors.

Throughout His ministry Jesus would consistently use the word *Father* when communicating to His listeners. In the Gospel of John the word *Father* was recorded more than 90 times. One of the main thrusts of Jesus' mission on earth was to reconcile mankind to their Father God. The title "Father" superceded all previous revelations of Jehovah; Jesus gave it pre-eminence over every other designation for God. Jesus' introduction of the name "Father" created a tidal wave of a completely new understanding of the Lord God, and it inspired men to seek Him with new fervor.

It is important for us to understand that Jesus was not just looking for a word that would help man to interpret God. He was not purporting an anthropological model to explain the unexplainable Almighty. The word *Father*, in its most sublime and noble sense, is the essence of who God is. It is intrinsic to His nature and unique to His relationship with the creation. Out of His Father-heart mankind was birthed. He was, is, and always shall be initiator, creator, protector, lover, provider, sustainer, and the beginning and end of all things.

> "Nay, the fatherhood which Scripture predicates of God is not something which God is *like*, but something which He essentially is. The really startling fact is this, that instead of the living fatherhood being a reflection of human fatherhood, it is human fatherhood which is an intended reflection of the divine!"[2]

In His historic sermon in the Gospel of Matthew, Jesus used the word *Father* 15 times.

> *But you, when you pray, go into your inner room, and when you have shut your door, pray to your **Father who is in secret**, and your Father who sees in secret will repay you* (Matthew 6:6).

> *Therefore do not be like them; **for your Father knows** what you need, before you ask Him* (Matthew 6:8).

2.   J. Sidlow Baxter, *Majesty, The God You Should Know* (San Bernardino, California: Here's Life Publishers, 1984), 169.

*Pray, then, in this way: "**Our Father who art in heaven**, hallowed be Thy name"* (Matthew 6:9).

*For if you forgive men for their transgressions, **your heavenly Father will also forgive you*** (Matthew 6:14).

*Look at the birds of the air, that they do not sow, neither do they reap, nor gather into barns, and yet your **heavenly Father feeds them**. Are you not worth much more than they?* (Matthew 6:26)

*For all these things the Gentiles eagerly seek; for your heavenly **Father knows that you need all these things*** (Matthew 6:32).

Jesus manifested this zeal for the Father at an early age as a young boy. His parents made it their custom to go up every year to Jerusalem so they could celebrate the Feast of Passover. The year Jesus turned 12, as they did every year, the family made their customary pilgrimage to the holy city. But this time, while on their way home, they realized that their son was not with them and frantically hurried back to Jerusalem to find their missing child. For three days they searched every conceivable corner of the city. Finally they located Him in the temple, amazingly dialoguing with the priests as their equal. His mother, who by this time was most likely exhausted from fear and worry, spoke harshly as she questioned Him about this treatment of His parents. The God/Man child turned to her and with calm perplexity asked, "Why is it that you were looking for Me? Did you not know that I had to be in My Father's house?"[3] The literal Greek reads, "Did you not know that I must be (busy) in the (affairs) of My Father?"[4]

"I must be about the things of My Father." This sentiment would distinguish Jesus' ministry from beginning to end. In the heart of the Incarnate Son was a determination and a drive to accomplish the Father's work and to reveal His ways in the short time available to Him. This passion would dominate His earthly ministry.

With perfect clarity Jesus reveals the substantive nature of the Father, and with fervent resolution He executes His Divine Will. From the beginning He made it His task to tear down all strongholds of deception and disillusionment concerning Father God. His very incarnate Being would

---

3.   Luke 2:49.
4.   Jay Green, *Interlinear Greek-English New Testament* (Grand Rapids, Michigan: Baker Book House, 1980), 82.

reflect the life qualities of His Father. His short human life stands as the watershed of mankind's history to understanding the true nature of God.

In the Upper Room Philip would ask that immortal question, "Lord, *show us the Father, and it is enough for us.*" Jesus replied, "Have I been so long with you, and yet you have not come to know Me, Philip? He *who has seen Me has seen the Father,* how do you say, 'Show us the Father'?"[5] Jesus was profoundly disappointed that Philip had not yet grasped this vital point. Philip had walked with the Master for three years. He had heard the words, seen the works, and felt the nearness of Heaven; yet he had failed to comprehend Jesus' life mission.

In the first chapter of John's Gospel, the apostle of the Lamb would declare with inspired conviction:

And the Word became flesh, and dwelt among us, and we beheld His glory, glory as of the only begotten from the Father, full of grace and truth....No man has seen God at any time; the only begotten God, who is in the bosom of the Father, He has explained Him (John 1:14,18).

Jesus' passion for the Father was founded on His uniqueness as the only Son of the Father. In His pre-incarnate existence, He was the darling Son of Father God, the "apple of His eye." As the "only Son," He enjoyed a depth of relationship with His Father that was beyond the scope and comprehension of the human mind. Looking on as a spectator, John vividly depicted the intimacy of that relationship with these words: *bosom of the Father.*

The dining custom amongst the Jews of that day was not to eat sitting at a table as we do; instead, they ate while in a reclining position. The dining table was formed by placing three separate tables in the formation of a square, with cushions set on the floor around the tables. The guests would recline on their left sides on these cushions, with their feet extended. In this position, their heads would naturally rest on the bosom of the one next to them.

" 'In the bosom of another' was an oriental phrase used to describe a very personal and tender relationship. It denotes intimacy, friendship and affection."[6] Jesus had an intimate knowledge of God that transcended any knowledge the Jewish leaders had. That knowledge proceeded from this

5.   John 14:8-9.

6.   Albert Barnes, *Barnes Notes on the New Testament* (Grand Rapids, Michigan: Kregel Publications, 1962), 108.

most intimate place. While those temple leaders pontificated on the acts of God, Jesus experienced a personal understanding of the Father's character, designs, and nature. Those Jews had not lived in His Presence. Nor had they observed firsthand His creative acts, redemptive works, or historical inter-actions with man.

Jesus' fiery zeal for the Father's work burned passionately in His inner-most being. As one "sent by the Father," Jesus articulated with picturesque profundity on the character of Father. With precision He detailed His Father's concealed peculiarities and demonstrated His compassionate pur-poses. An intimacy of knowledge was shared between the Father and His Son. With ecstatic joy the Son would disclose those secrets of Father God to the family of man.

The Father loves the Son.

Jesus' devotion to the Father is fueled by the profound love affair that exists between Father and Son. It is clear that the Father deeply loves the Son. The Son has the full attention of the Father. "Other things" never dis-tract Jesus. He is consistently in tune with the love the Father shows Him.

The Father loves the Son, and has given all things into His hand (John 3:35).

For the Father loves the Son, and shows Him all things that He Himself is doing; and greater works than these will He show Him, that you may marvel (John 5:20).

Because of that great love, the Father has placed the totality of His Divine, eternal purpose into the hands of the Son. He trusts the Son implic-itly to carry out the desires of His heart. Father rests in His love and trust for the Son. Therefore, He pulls back the veil between the spirit realm and the physical, allowing the Son to see the work of the Father. To the deep gratification of the Father, the Son reciprocates with His own response of passionate love. The Son longs to perpetually live in the Presence of the Father, and He wholeheartedly commits Himself to the work of the Father.

He who has My commandments and keeps them, he it is who loves Me; and he who loves Me shall be loved by My Father, and I will love him, and will disclose Myself to him (John 14:21).

Just as the Father has loved Me, I have also loved you; abide in My love (John 15:9).

What awesome words! Jesus invites the disciples to participate in the fellowship of that love. As He obeys the Father in all things, so too the disciples are invited to enter through the door of obedient submission to the will of the Father and into that circle of love.

The Father who is in Heaven.

In order that you may be sons of your Father who is in heaven; for He causes His sun to rise on the evil and the good, and sends rain on the righteous and the unrighteous (Matthew 5:45).

Beware of practicing your righteousness before men to be noticed by them; otherwise you have no reward with your Father who is in heaven (Matthew 6:1).

That your alms may be in secret; and your Father who sees in secret will repay you (Matthew 6:4).

But you, when you pray, go into your inner room, and when you have shut your door, pray to your Father who is in secret, and your Father who sees in secret will repay you (Matthew 6:6).

Not everyone who says to Me, "Lord, Lord," will enter the kingdom of heaven; but he who does the will of My Father who is in heaven (Matthew 7:21).

Heaven is the dwelling place of the Father...the location of His throne...the habitation for His Presence. Every family must have a home, for their home is the center of their activities. It is the expression of who the family is in community. For our heavenly Father, Heaven is His home.

Heaven is the center of the invisible realm in which God lives. Heaven is the place where the fullness of Father's Presence is manifested. Every Divine activity on earth proceeds from Heaven, but His Presence is only in "testimony" here on the earth. To address God is to address Him in Heaven: "Our Father who art in heaven...."[7] Heaven is His place of residence. It is the place where He is most comfortable, and it is filled with angelic worship and perfect harmony. Heaven is characterized by perfect rest and glorious symmetry.

———————————

7.　Matthew 6:9.

Men are trying to get to Heaven while God is trying to get Heaven to men. It is the will of the Father to relate everything on earth to Heaven. "Thy kingdom come. Thy will be done, on earth as it is in heaven."[8] The Son comes as the full expression of Heaven, representing Heaven in its fullest import. *He comes to establish Heaven's rule in the affairs of man.*

> "The Bible teaches us that God is located in heaven. 'God is in heaven,' (Ecc 5:2): that is the declaration. It teaches that there is a system, an order, in heaven, which is the true one and which is the ultimate one. In the end, it will be the reproduction of a heavenly order upon this earth which will be the consummation of all the counsels of God. Christ came down from heaven and returned to heaven."[9]

Father has life in Himself.

As Father, He is the Giver and the Sustainer of all life. In the Garden He gave man his beginning by breathing into him the breath of His life. It is that life that authenticates man, animating the body, energizing the soul, and quickening the spirit. The Father is the One who supports and gives meaning to that life. Unconscious of that sustaining power, man nevertheless finds his place in creation. Although not always aware of it, man is solely dependent upon the upholding influence of that Divine life force. One word from the Father, and the flame can be extinguished and the life go out.

One axiom of human life is this: Nothing is complete in itself. All created life depends on the environment in which it lives for water, air, food, and even sunlight. God is the source of that life, but He needs *no* thing. God is complete in Himself, existing independent of His creation. The beginning of all things exists in Him. He is the Divine Initiator and every thing that is, owes its existence to the Father.

Not only is the Father the source of all life, but He also is the One who infuses quality into that life. He transforms a life of mere existence into one filled with dynamic joyful living and focused purpose. He sent His Son into the world to be the carrier of that Divine Life.

In Him was life, and the life was the light of men (John 1:4).

---

8. Matthew 6:10.
9. T. Austin-Sparks, *Pioneers of the Heavenly Way* (Gaithersburg, Maryland: Testimony Book Ministry, n.d.), 9.

For just as the Father has life in Himself, even so He gave to the Son also to have life in Himself (John 5:26).

As the living Father sent Me, and I live because of the Father, so he who eats Me, he also shall live because of Me (John 6:57).

And this is eternal life, that they may know Thee, the only true God, and Jesus Christ whom Thou hast sent (John 17:3).

Tragically, ever since man rejected the Father of life in the Garden of Eden, choosing knowledge instead, the quality of his life has been cheapened. Jesus made an unrestrained commitment to bridge the gap between the sterile subsistence of the human race and the substantive significance of the Divine Life. He entered the human race with the power of that eternal Life resident within Him, and He freely offers it to any and all who will call upon His name.

Father knows best.

For all these things the Gentiles eagerly seek; for your heavenly Father knows that you need all these things (Matthew 6:32).

All things have been handed over to Me by My Father; and no one knows the Son, except the Father; nor does anyone know the Father, except the Son, and anyone to whom the Son wills to reveal Him (Matthew 11:27).

But of that day and hour no one knows, not even the angels of heaven, nor the Son, but the Father alone (Matthew 24:36).

For all these things the nations of the world eagerly seek; but your Father knows that you need these things (Luke 12:30).

Even as the Father knows Me and I know the Father; and I lay down My life for the sheep (John 10:15).

Jesus made it clear from the beginning that the Father knows what is best for His creation. The wisdom and all-knowing power of God has been one of the inspirations for the myriad of theological expositions on the nature of the Father. We, as followers of the Son, do not search for theological explanations about God; rather, we seek the comforting security that comes from understanding that there is One who does know all things. We find solace throughout the pain and perplexities of life in the deep knowing that our Father understands what we need before we ever articulate a prayer. Peaceful confidence is ours, for the God who sees a small bird fall from its nest has His "eye" continually upon us.[10]

The Father, who lives outside of time, sees the end from the beginning; He has no need for conjecture or suppositions. His plans and provisions for man are not based upon a Divine hunch, but upon a plan conceived before the foundations of the earth. In His perfect wisdom Father weaves His perfect plans for His children with precision timing.

Man, on his own, does not have the benefit of the panoramic view of Father God. Instead he is guided by the eternal perspective of the One who lives outside of time as He works on behalf of His creation. That is why the Scriptures tell us that, without faith, no one can hope to see the Father.[11] With faith, we know that *because the Father knows best, the creation can be at rest*!

> "God knows instantly and effortlessly all matter and all matters, all mind and every mind, all spirit and all spirits, all being and every being, all creaturehood and all creatures, every plurality and all pluralities, all law and every law, all relations, all causes, all thoughts, all mysteries, all enigmas, all feeling, all desires, every unuttered secret, all thrones and dominions, all personalities, all things visible and invisible in heaven and in earth, motion, space, time, life, death, good, evil, heaven and hell.

> "Because God knows all things perfectly, He knows no thing better than any other thing, but all things equally well. He never discovers anything. He is never surprised, never amazed. He never wonders about anything nor (except when drawing men out for their own good) does he seek information or ask questions."[12]

Father is always at work.

Empowered by His revelation of the Father's nature, Jesus set about establishing the Father's work. Just as the Father does not sit on the "easy chair" of His throne, directing the work of others, neither does the Son. As Gene Edwards says, "He is a blue-collar God." Jesus passionately gave Himself to the work of the Father. His agenda was vitally linked with the will of His Father.

---

10. See Matthew 6.
11. See Hebrews 11:6.
12. A.W. Tozer, *The Knowledge of the Holy* (New York: Harper & Row, 1961), 62-63.

But He answered them, "My Father is working until now, and I Myself am working" (John 5:17).

Jesus therefore answered and was saying to them, "Truly, truly, I say to you, the Son can do nothing of Himself, unless it is something He sees the Father doing; for whatever the Father does, these things the Son also does in like manner. For the Father loves the Son, and shows Him all things that He Himself is doing; and greater works than these will He show Him, that you may marvel" (John 5:19-20).

Jesus answered them, "I showed you many good works from the Father; for which of them are you stoning Me?" (John 10:32)

Do you not believe that I am in the Father, and the Father is in Me? The words that I say to you I do not speak on My own initiative, but the Father abiding in Me does His works (John 14:10).

In the beginning of time, God worked for six days and rested on the seventh. The first day of man began in the rest of God. Jesus knew how to labor in the "rest" of God.

With great resolve Jesus asserted that He did only what He saw the Father doing. There are two things in this statement that vie for our attention.

First, the Father is always at work. He did not set the world in motion and then step back to remain a disinterested bystander. Father God remains actively involved in the affairs of His creation. The Scriptures are a written account of the continuous activity of God in the ongoing history of mankind.

The creative work of Father was first recorded in the Book of Genesis. With an artistic exhibition of sovereign action, He formed a world that was to be the living stage for expressing His will and nature in a time/space continuum. Man was the being created to occupy the center of that stage as the object of the Father's compassionate work.

The fall of man in the Garden becomes the setting for the next manifested work of the Father: the work of redemption. The Old Testament recounts the initiation of that redemptive work. Jehovah calls Abraham to be the "father of Israel"; generations later He chooses Moses to lead Israel out of the bondage of Egypt; still later He leads Joshua and the children of Israel into the land of promise—their place of inheritance on this earth. He anoints deliverers to rescue Israel from one enemy after another. He establishes the throne of David for the promised coming King. He speaks through the prophets. Our God is and always has been a God at work.

In the fullness of time through the Person of His beloved Son, the Father consummates the work of redeeming man back from his slave master, satan, to his original purpose. The full expression of the work of God is demonstrated in the acts of the Son of Man. Jesus passionately persisted in accomplishing every singular detail of the work that Father had entrusted into His hands. When the Son came to the end of His earthly mission, He could accurately declare, "It is finished!"

The second thing that strikes us in Jesus' statement of John 5:19-20 is His ability to see what the Father is doing. His spirit was fixed moment by moment on the Father, who always moved His Son in the direction and the focus of His work. Jesus' daily schedule was in the hands of the Father; His agenda for His work in the spirit realm was fixed by Father's word. The key to the unqualified success of the Son's ministry lay in doing on earth what He saw His Father doing in the realm of the spirit.

The priests and religious leaders of Jesus' day went about blindly doing their religious duties, totally oblivious to the workings of the Father. They were prisoners of their own self-created tasks and were spiritually blinded by their commitment to fulfill their personal agendas.

The Father is always looking for a man or woman who will cooperate with Him in the Divine work. The key to true spiritual ministry with fruit that remains is to perceive what God is doing in the spiritual realm and then manifest it in the physical realm.

When He finds someone who discerns, by the Spirit, His heart and eternal purposes, He empowers that person with the spiritual and physical resources to accomplish His will on earth. The Son is our perfect role model of One who consistently and accurately replicated the work of the Father in this life.

> *If I do not do the works of My Father, do not believe Me; but if I do them, though you do not believe Me, believe the works, that you may know and understand that the Father is in Me, and I in the Father* (John 10:37-38).

Jesus' works were living testimonials to the active work of the Father and to the union that existed between Father and Son. No man can do the works that Jesus did unless he is empowered by the Father to do them. During His final days, while with His disciples, Jesus promised those budding apostles that they would do not only the works they had witnessed Him do, but even greater acts because He was going to be with the Father and would intercede for them.

Truly, truly, I say to you, he who believes in Me, the works that I do shall he do also; and greater works than these shall he do; because I go to the Father (John 14:12).

Father is ever searching for the man who will abandon his own agenda to pursue the true work of God. Through undoubting faith and abandoned obedience, the follower of the Son can also enter into joyous cooperation with the activity of God in the world. Unfortunately, too many in Father's Kingdom seek their own work with never an inkling of what He is doing. They presume that because they are continually doing some good thing, they must be doing the work of God. We are too busy if we never take time to pause and consider that we just might not be doing the work of God but living out our own plans and ambitions through unrelenting striving in the flesh.

Father waits for the return of the Son.

I came forth from the Father, and have come into the world; I am leaving the world again, and going to the Father (John 16:28).

Jesus said to her, "Stop clinging to Me, for I have not yet ascended to the Father; but go to My brethren, and say to them, 'I ascend to My Father and your Father, and My God and your God' " (John 20:17).

Jesus proceeded from the Father, and He knew that one day He would go back home to the Father. The Father's heart was always anticipating the triumphant return of the Son. The throne was prepared for the Lamb that was slain, and it would remain empty until that bloodstained One would sit down upon it, to the joy of Heaven's hosts.

Now the moment of departure is at hand. Parting is such sweet sorrow! Jesus must soon leave the disciples whom He has come to so dearly love. He must "ascend" to His Father in order to oversee the final outworkings of the work He has initiated. The veil that separated the Creator from His creation is now rent. From His throne at the right hand of the Father the Son will now oversee—through those to whom He imparted His passions—the building of His Church, the expansion of His Kingdom, and the culmination of the ages.

But to do this He must first return to the Father. For 33 years Heaven quietly mourned the absence of the only begotten Son. Jesus can surely feel the anticipation building as He contemplates His return. He knows that a coronation awaits Him...that the fullness of joy will fill the heavenly courts at His triumphant return.

Notice again in John 20:17 His words, "to My Father and your Father." He has broadened the exclusive relationship that He enjoyed with Father God. Man can now be included in that father/son relationship. Man is invited to relinquish his servant role for the privileged position of a son.

Before Jesus ascends, He tells His disciples that He will send the "promise of the Father" to be their Instructor.[13] The Son will commission the Holy Spirit to serve and to teach His beloved disciples. The Holy Spirit will be their tutor and train them in the etiquette of sonship. There is much that they must learn if they too will be true sons of the Father. The Holy Spirit will tenderly and relentlessly educate them and equip them to walk as heirs of Heaven. Life will become the training ground to prepare sons of the Kingdom to reign with the eternal Son. When these simple, humble men each approach the close of their earthly lives, the promise that their Master gave to them of reigning one day with Him imparts an ever-increasing anticipation of a joyous "home-coming." Their thrones are waiting and the Son is watching for these faithful ones to return to their Father!

While St. Ignatius of Antioch was on his way to martyrdom (he was taken from Asia Minor to Rome to be martyred in the circus of Nero), he wrote letters to the various Christian communities as he passed through them, encouraging them in living the Christian life. But the letter he wrote to the church in Rome was a little different. He begged them not to use their influence to save him from martyrdom. He knew that certain Christians in the church of Rome lived in the imperial household and had certain influence, and could perhaps save him. He didn't want them to do that. He says, "My lust has been crucified, and there is no fire of material

---

13.   See Acts 2:33.

longing in me, but only water living and speaking in me, saying within me, Come to the Father."[14]

---

14.   J.B. Lightfoot, *The Apostolic Fathers* (Grand Rapids, Michigan: Baker Book House, first printing 1956), 78.

Chapter 6

Part II

Going to the Father[1]

Henry Drummond was born in Stirling, Scotland, in 1851. He became a close friend of Dwight L. Moody and assisted him in his religious campaigns, which led to a religious revival on an unprecedented scale. Henry was a preacher of extraordinary power and sincerity and a writer without equal. His friend, Ian Maclaren, described him this way:

"Just as there are periods in the development of Christianity, there are men in every age corresponding to each of the periods—modern, Reformation, and Mediaeval minds—and what charmed many in Drummond was this, that he belonged by nature to the pre-theological age. He was in his habit and thought a Christian of the Gospels, rather than of the Epistles, and preferred to walk with Jesus in Galilee rather than argue with Judaizers and Gnostics. It would be a gross injustice to say that he was anti-theological: it would be correct to say that he was non-theological. Jesus was not to him an official Redeemer discharging certain obligations: He was his unseen Friend with Whom he walked in life, by Whose fellowship he was changed, to Whom he prayed. The effort of life should be to do the

---

1.   Henry Drummond, "Going to the Father," *The Ideal Life and Other Unpublished Addresses* (London: Hodder & Stoughton, 1897). 1998. October 1, 1999. <http://ccel.wheaton.edu/ d/drummond/ideal life/ideal05.htm/>. Public domain. Reprinted as is.

Will of God, the strength of life was Peace, the reward of life was to be like Jesus. Perfect Christianity was to be as St. John was with Jesus. It was the Idyll of Religion."[2]

In this classic writing by Henry Drummond, we are introduced to the fact that the great design of Heaven is to bring everything "back to the Father." There is no life worth living if it is not a life that is returning to the Father.

*   *   *

Henry Drummond

"I go to my Father."—JOHN xiv. 12.

WRITTEN AFTER THE DEATH OF A FRIEND

You can unlock a man's whole life if you watch what words he uses most. We have each a small set of words, which, though we are scarce aware of it, we always work with, and which really express all that we mean by life, or have found out of it. For such words embalm the past for us. They have become ours by a natural selection throughout our career of all that is richest and deepest in our experience. So our vocabulary is our history, and our favourite words are ourselves.

Did you ever notice Christ's favourite words? If you have you must have been struck by two things—their simplicity and their fewness. Some half-dozen words embalm all his theology and these are, without exception, humble, elementary, simple monosyllables. They are such words as these—world, life, trust, love.

But none of these was the greatest word of Christ. His great word was new to religion. There was no word there, when He came, rich enough to carry the new truth He was bringing to men. So He imported into religion one of the grandest words of human language, and transfigured it, and gave it back to the world illuminated and transformed, as the watchword of the new religion. That word was Father.

---

2.   From the Memorial Sketch in Henry Drummond, *The Ideal Life and Other Unpublished Addresses* (London: Hodder & Stoughton, 1897). 1998. October 1, 1999. <http://ccel.wheaton.edu/d/drummond/ideal life/ideal05.htm/>.

The world's obligation to the Lord Jesus is that He gave us that word. We should never have thought of it—if we had, we should never have dared to say it. It is a pure revelation. Surely it is the most touching sight of the world's past to see God's only begotten Son coming down from heaven to try to teach the stammering dumb inhabitants of this poor planet to say, "Our Father."

It is that word which has gathered the great family of God together; and when we come face to face with the real, the solid, and the moving in our religion, it is to find all its complexity resolvable into this simplicity, that God, whom others call King Eternal, Infinite Jehovah, is, after all, our Father, and we are His children.

This, after all, is religion. And to live daily in this simplicity, is to live like Christ.

It takes a great deal to succeed as a Christian—such a great deal, that not many do succeed. And the great reason for want of success is the want of a central word. Men will copy anything rather than a principle. A relationship is always harder to follow than a fact. We study the details of Christ's actions, the point of this miracle and of that, the circumferential truth of this parable and of that, but to copy details is not to copy Christ. To live greatly like Christ is not to agonize daily over details, to make anxious comparisons with what we do and what He did, but a much more simple thing. It is to re-echo Christ's word. It is to have that calm, patient, assured spirit, which reduces life simply to this— a going to the Father.

Not one man in a hundred, probably, has a central word in his Christian life; and the consequence is this, that there is probably nothing in the world so disorderly and slipshod as personal spiritual experience. With most of us it is a thing without stability or permanence, it is changed by every trifle we meet, by each new mood or thought. It is a series of disconnected approaches to God, a disorderly succession of religious impulses, an irregulation of conduct, now on this principle, now on that, one day because we read something in a book, the next because it was contradicted in another. And when circumstances lead us really to examine ourselves, everything is indefinite, hazy, unsatisfactory, and all that we have for the Christian life are the shreds perhaps of the last few Sabbaths' sermons and a few borrowed patches from other people's experience. So we live in perpetual spiritual oscillation and confusion, and we are almost glad to let any friend or any book upset the most cherished thought we have.

Now the thing which steadied Christ's life was the thought that He was going to His Father. This one thing gave it unity, and harmony, and success. During His whole life He never forgot His Word for a moment. There is no sermon of His where it does not occur; there is no prayer, however brief, where it is missed. In that first memorable sentence of His, which breaks the solemn spell of history and makes one word resound through thirty silent years, the one word is this; and all through the after years of toil and travail "the Great Name" was always hovering on His lips, or bursting out of His heart. In its beginning and in its end, from the early time when He spoke of His Father's business till He finished the work that was given Him to do, His life, disrobed of all circumstance, was simply this, "I go to My Father."

If we take this principle into our own lives, we shall find its influence tell upon us in three ways:

I. It explains Life.

II. It sustains Life.

III. It completes Life.

I. It explains Life. Few men, I suppose, do not feel that life needs explaining. We think we see through some things in it— partially; but most of it, even to the wisest mind, is enigmatic. Those who know it best are the most bewildered by it, and they who stand upon the mere rim of the vortex confess that even for them it is overspread with cloud and shadow. What is my life? whither do I go? whence do I come? these are the questions which are not worn down yet, although the whole world has handled them.

To these questions there are but three answers—one by the poet, the other by the atheist, the third by the Christian.

(a) The poet tells us, and philosophy says the same, only less intelligibly, that life is a sleep, a dream, a shadow. It is a vapour that appeareth for a little and vanisheth away; a meteor hovering for a moment between two unknown eternities; bubbles, which form and burst upon the river of time. This philosophy explains nothing. It is a taking refuge in mystery. Whither am I going? Virtually the poet answers, "I am going to the Unknown."

(b) The atheist's answer is just the opposite. He knows no unknown. He understands all, for there is nothing more than we can see or feel. Life is what matter is, the soul is phosphorus. Whither am I going? "I go to dust," he says; "death ends all." And this explains nothing. It is worse than mystery. It is contradiction. It is utter darkness.

(c) But the Christian's answer explains something. Where is he going? "I go to my Father." This is not a definition of his death—there is no death in Christianity; it is a definition of the Christian life. All the time it is a going to the Father. Some travel swiftly, some are long upon the road, some meet many pleasant adventures by the way, others pass through fire and peril; but though the path be short or winding, and though the pace be quick or slow, it is a going to the Father.

Now this explains life. It explains the two things in life which are most inexplicable. For one thing, it explains why there is more pain in the world than pleasure. God knows, although we scarce do, there is something better than pleasure—progress. Pleasure, mere pleasure, is animal. He gives that to the butterfly. But progress is the law of life to the immortal. So God has arranged our life as progress, and its working principle is evolution. Not that there is no pleasure in it. The Father is too good to His children for that. But the shadows are all shot through it, for He fears lest we should forget there is anything more. Yes, God is too good to leave His children without indulgences, without far more than we deserve; but He is too good to let them spoil us. Our pleasures therefore are mere entertainments. We are entertained like passing guests at the inns on the roadside. Yet after even the choicest meals we dare not linger. We must take the pilgrim's staff again and go on our way to the Father.

Sooner or later we find out that life is not a holiday, but a discipline. Earlier or later we all discover that the world is not a playground. It is quite clear God means it for a school. The moment we forget that, the puzzle of life begins. We try to play in school; the Master does not mind that so much for its own sake, for He likes to see His children happy, but in our playing we neglect our lessons. We do not see how much there is to learn, and we do not care. But our Master cares. He has a perfectly overpowering and inexplicable solicitude for our education; and because He loves us, He comes into the school sometimes and speaks to us. He may speak very softly and gently, or very loudly. Sometimes a look is enough, and we understand it, like Peter, and go out at once and weep bitterly. Sometimes the voice is like a thunderclap startling a summer night. But one thing we may be sure of: the task He sets us to is never measured by our delinquency. The discipline may seem far less than our desert, or even to our eye ten times more. But it is not measured by these—it is measured by God's solicitude for our progress; measured solely by God's love; measured solely that the scholar may be better educated when he arrives at his Father. The discipline of life is a preparation for meeting the Father. When we arrive there to behold His beauty, we must have the educated eye; and that must be trained here. We must become so pure in heart—and it needs much practice—that we shall see God. That explains life—why God puts man in the crucible and makes him pure by fire.

When we see Him, we must speak to Him. We have that language to learn. And that is perhaps why God makes us pray so much. Then we are to walk with Him in white. Our sanctification is a putting on this white. But there has to be much disrobing first; much putting off of filthy rags. This is why God makes man's beauty to consume away like the moth. He takes away the moth's wings, and gives the angel's, and man goes the quicker and the lovelier to the Father.

It is quite true, indeed, besides all this, that sometimes shadow falls more directly from definite sin. But even then its explanation is the same. We lose our way, perhaps, on the way to the Father. The road is rough, and we choose the way with the flowers beside it, instead of the path of thorns. Often and often thus, purposely or carelessly, we lose the way. So the Lord Jesus has to come and look for us. And He may have to lead us through desert and danger, before we regain the road—before we are as we were—and the voice says to us sadly once more, "This is the way to the Father."

The other thing which this truth explains is, why there is so much that is unexplained. After we have explained all, there is much left. All our knowledge, it is said, is but different degrees of darkness. But we know why we do not know why. It is because we are going to our Father. We are only going: we are not there yet. Therefore patience. "What I do thou knowest not now, but thou shalt know. Hereafter, thou shalt know." Hereafter, because the chief joy of life is to have something to look forward to. But, hereafter, for a deeper reason. Knowledge is only given for action. Knowing only exists for doing: and already nearly all men know to do more than they do do. So, till we do all that we know, God retains the balance till we can use it. In the larger life of the hereafter, more shall be given, proportionate to the vaster sphere and the more ardent energies.

Necessarily, therefore, much of life is still twilight. But our perfect refuge is to anticipate a little and go in thought to our Father, and, like children tired out with efforts to put together the disturbed pieces of a puzzle, wait to take the fragments to our Father.

And yet, even that fails sometimes. He seems to hide from us and the way is lost indeed. The footsteps which went before us up till then cease, and we are left in the chill, dark night alone. If we could only see the road, we should know it went to the Father. But we cannot say we are going to the Father; we can only say we would like to go. "Lord," we cry, "we know not whither thou goest, and how can we know the way?" "Whither I go," is the inexplicable answer, "ye know not now." Well is it for those who at such times are near enough to catch the rest: "But ye shall know hereafter."

II. Secondly, and in a few words, this sustains Life.

A year or two ago some of the greatest and choicest minds of this country laboured, in the pages of one of our magazines, to answer the question, "Is Life worth living?" It was a triumph for religion, some thought, that the keenest intellects of the nineteenth century should be stirred with themes like this. It was not so; it was the surest proof of the utter heathenism of our age. Is Life worth living? As well ask, Is air worth breathing? The real question is this—taking the definition of life here suggested—Is it worth while going to the Father?

Yet we can understand the question. On any other definition we can understand it. On any other definition life is very far from being worth living. Without that, life is worse than an enigma; it is an inquisition. Life is either a discipline, or a most horrid cruelty. Man's best aims here are persistently thwarted, his purest aspirations degraded, his intellect systematically insulted, his spirit of inquiry is crushed, his love mocked, and his hope stultified. There is no solution whatever to life without this; there is nothing to sustain either mind or soul amid its terrible mystery but this; there is nothing even to account for mind and soul. And it will always be a standing miracle that men of powerful intellect who survey life, who feel its pathos and bitterness, and are shut up all the time by their beliefs to impenetrable darkness—I say it will always be a standing miracle how such men, with the terrible unsolved problems all around them, can keep reason from reeling and tottering from its throne. If life is not a going to the Father, it is not only not worth living, it is an insult to the living; and it is one of the strangest mysteries how men who are large enough in one direction to ask that question, and too limited in another to answer it, should voluntarily continue to live at all.

There is nothing to sustain life but this thought. And it does sustain life. Take even an extreme case, and you will see how. Take the darkest, saddest, most pathetic life of the world's history. That was Jesus Christ's. See what this truth practically was to Him. It gave Him a life of absolute composure in a career of most tragic trials.

You have noticed often, and it is inexpressibly touching, how as His life narrows, and troubles thicken around Him, He leans more and more upon this. And when the last days draw near—as the memorable chapters in John reveal them to us—with what clinging tenderness He alludes in almost every second sentence to "My Father." There is a wistful eagerness in these closing words which is strangely melting—like one ending a letter at sea when land is coming into sight.

This is the Christian's only stay in life. It provides rest for his soul, work for his character, an object, an inconceivably sublime object, for his ambition. It does not stagger him to be a stranger here, to feel the world passing away. The Christian is like the pearl-diver, who is out of the sunshine for a little, spending his short day amid rocks and weeds and dangers at the bottom of the ocean. Does he desire to spend his life there? No, but his Master does. Is his life there? No, his life is up above. A communication is open to the surface, and the fresh pure life comes down to him from God. Is he not wasting time there? He is gathering pearls for his Master's crown. Will he always stay there? When the last pearl is gathered, the "Come up higher" will beckon him away, and the weights which kept him down will become an exceeding weight of glory, and he will go, he and those he brings with him, to his Father.

He feels, to change the metaphor, like a man in training for a race. It is months off still, but it is nearer him than to-morrow, nearer than anything else. Great things are always near things. So he lives in his future. Ask him why this deliberate abstinence from luxury in eating and drinking. "He is keeping his life," he says. Why this self-denial, this separation from worldliness, this change to a quiet life from revelries far into the night? "He is keeping his life." He cannot have both the future and the present; and he knows that every regulated hour, and every temptation scorned and set aside, is adding a nobler tissue to his frame and keeping his life for the prize that is to come.

Trial to the Christian is training for eternity, and he is perfectly contented; for he knows that "he who loveth his life in this world shall lose it—but he that hateth his life in this world shall keep it unto life eternal." He is keeping his life till he gets to the Father.

III. Lastly, in a word, this completes life.

Life has been defined as a going to the Father. It is quite clear that there must come a time in the history of all those who live this life when they reach the Father. This is the most glorious moment of life. Angels attend at it. Those on the other side must hail the completing of another soul with ineffable rapture. When they are yet a great way off, the Father runs and falls on their neck and kisses them.

On this side we call that Death. It means reaching the Father. It is not departure, it is arrival; not sleep, but waking. For life to those who live like Christ is not a funeral procession. It is a triumphal march to the Father. And the entry at the last in God's own chariot is the best hour of all. No, as we watch a life which is going to the Father, we cannot think of night, of gloom, of dusk and sunset. It is life which is the night, and Death is sunrise.

"Pray moderately," says an old saint, "for the lives of Christ's people." Pray moderately. We may want them on our side, he means, but Christ may need them on His. He has seen them a great way off, and set His heart upon them, and asked the Father to make them come quickly. "I will," He says, "that such an one should be with Me where I am." So it is better that they should go to the Father.

These words have a different emphasis to different persons. There are three classes to whom they come home with a peculiar emphasis:—

1. They speak to those who are staying away from God. "I do not wonder at what men suffer," says Ruskin, "I wonder often at what they lose." My fellow pilgrim, you do not know what you are losing by not going to the Father. You live in an appalling mystery. You have nothing to explain your life, nor to sustain it; no boundary line on the dim horizon to complete it. When life is done you are going to leap into the dark. You will cross the dark river and land on the further shore alone. No one will greet you. You and the Inhabitant of Eternity will be strangers. Will you not to-day arise and go to your Father?

2. They speak, next, to all God's people. Let us remember that we are going to the Father. Even now are we the sons of God. Oh, let us live like it—more simple, uncomplaining, useful, separate—joyful as those who march with music, yet sober as those who are to company with Christ. The road is heavy, high road and low road, but we shall soon be home. God grant us a sure arrival in our Father's house.

3. And this voice whispers yet one more message to the mourning. Did Death end all? Is it well with the child? It is well. The last inn by the roadside has been passed—that is all, and a voice called to us. "Good-bye! I go to my Father."

Chapter 7

The Passion for the Disinherited

IN ETERNITY PAST, while enjoying the fellowship of His angelic hosts, the ever-living One determined that He would have another life form with whom He could enjoy unending communion. So He created man, gave him a setting of untold beauty, and walked and talked with him in harmonious, heartfelt intimacy.

The entrance of sin, while disrupting His plan, did not defeat it. God was committed to this being that He had created; He let it be known to the principalities and powers that He Himself would, at a predetermined time, intervene and rescue this being from the destruction he had unleashed on earth. He would not, in disappointment and anger, wipe his very memory from the slate of eternity; instead, He would give up a part of Himself as expiation for that sin, which had to be satisfied. He would step out of the shroud of mystery that obscured Him from man and unveil Himself to the world in the Person of His Son.

John 3:16 tells us that because of the great love the Father had for His creation, He sent His beloved Son. The mission to earth was launched from the platform of Heaven. Jesus entered the human race consumed with the zeal of His Father and with the fire of that love blazing in every fiber of His being. He *would* see the plan of the Second Adam fulfilled.

From the eternal warmth of the "communion of glory" with His Father, the Son of Man descended into the cold abyss of human misery. This holy strategy necessarily included His being stripped of any Divine advantage. He exited through the bright light of Heaven's gate—an exit witnessed by the consternation of hosts of angels—and entered into the misery and hopelessness that circumscribed the existence of humankind.

By the time Jesus entered the human race, the nation of Israel had a tragic history of having abandoned the precepts and laws that God gave them through His servant Moses—laws that ensured their relationship with Him. Among these lost precepts was the care of the poor and downtrodden. The nation's advantaged, with their religious superiority, arrogant pride, love of riches, and lust for position, had become blinded to the glaring needs of the hurting among them. Legalistic interpretations of the law had left the poor, sick, and disadvantaged on the outer fringes of Jewish society. The Jewish faith had deteriorated into an elitist system that entrenched the rich and religious leaders firmly at the top and abandoned the rest of the nation to live at the bottom, carrying the burden of their own pain and suffering.

Severe laws were harshly enforced against the company of lepers. They were driven beyond the walls of the city and were forced to announce their coming with cries of "Unclean, unclean." Tax collectors were looked upon as a hateful blight on the Jewish culture; they were viewed as traitors to the Jewish cause. Women were relegated to the lowly role of servant to the male-dominated society. *Publicans* became the accepted catchall term for sinners who transgressed the oppressive laws laid down by the religious elite.

The spiritual community of Jesus' day had evolved into a caste society set up by the priestly aristocracy to eliminate the accessibility of the "defiled." The brotherhood of rabbis and priests constructed a wall that kept them safe from contamination by the dregs of the lower classes.

Onto this stage of despair strode the Son of God, preaching the good news of the Kingdom and offering spiritual life that was free to all who would reach out in faith. This hope could not be purchased by the wealth of the rich or attained by the position of the elite. It could be received only as a free gift by any who would humble himself and reach out to take it by faith.

He was tireless in His pursuit of bringing purpose and power to the people, hope to the hopeless, healing to the sick, an inheritance to the disinherited, and acceptance to the rejected. His strategy was to empower the company of the disenfranchised and bring down the oppressive religious order of the day.

The depth of Jesus' love for the poor and needy originated from the throne. We should not be surprised by His deep compassion for those who dwell on the fringes of human existence. Jesus came in the spirit of His Father—the spirit of love for the lost, care for the poor, and wholeness for the broken. He explained His mission when He said that He had come to seek and to save the lost.[1]

His heart for the poor and powerless extended all the way back to the establishment of the Jewish nation, when His Father instituted protective laws for the poor and unfortunate in its midst.

> *If you lend money to My people, to the poor among you, you are not to act as a creditor to him; you shall not charge him interest* (Exodus 22:25).

> *However, there shall be no poor among you, since the Lord will surely bless you in the land which the Lord your God is giving you as an inheritance to possess* (Deuteronomy 15:4).

> *He raises the poor from the dust, He lifts the needy from the ash heap to make them sit with nobles, and inherit a seat of honor; for the pillars of the earth are the Lord's, and He set the world on them* (1 Samuel 2:8).

> *So that they caused the cry of the poor to come to Him, and that He might hear the cry of the afflicted* (Job 34:28).

> *He will have compassion on the poor and needy, and the lives of the needy he will save* (Psalm 72:13).

> *He raises the poor from the dust, and lifts the needy from the ash heap* (Psalm 113:7).

> *I know that the Lord will maintain the cause of the afflicted, and justice for the poor* (Psalm 140:12).

> *He who is gracious to a poor man lends to the Lord, and He will repay him for his good deed* (Proverbs 19:17).

> *And do not oppress the widow or the orphan, the stranger or the poor; and do not devise evil in your hearts against one another* (Zechariah 7:10).

Many times the Gospel writers would record that Jesus "felt compassion." The words were penned with wonder. The Scriptures declare that God is love. Could it be that experiencing the Divine nature of God in a human body is one of the many mysteries of human experience that Jesus encountered in this mortal body? Love is not a foreign affection to the Eter-

---

1.   See Luke 19:10.

nal One. But, experiencing the power of its passion and the affinity of its affection in a human body might have at times overwhelmed the Son of Man. Again and again the swells of compassion and pain for the state of the lost sheep swept over Him as He walked in the midst of this anemic people.

When He saw the crowds, He had compassion on them, because they were harassed and helpless, like sheep without a shepherd (Matthew 9:36 NIV).

Jesus called His disciples to Him and said, "I have compassion for these people..." (Matthew 15:32 NIV).

The power of a compassionate touch is introduced by the Son of Man.

He could not and would not ignore this powerful emotion; He repeatedly submitted to its call for action. This compassion was felt by the One who had the power to reverse the curses of human sickness and societal devolution. He reached out and *"touched"* the unclean and the rejected. The power of the *touch* was introduced on earth by the Word Incarnate.

For the Jews the ministry of laying on of hands, if practiced at all, had been a perfunctory and ceremonial religious exercise devoid of any true emotion and most certainly of any power. But with Jesus, the *touch* was truly an expression of Divine Love and human compassion. It was an empathizing, caring action that manifested the heart of the Eternal God to restore the broken and heal the wounded. The *touch* was not symbolic; it was a heart response that was rich in Heaven's love and power. The touch of Jesus combined passionate affection with supernatural power.

Jesus became known far and wide for the power of His touch. Over and over again He reached out to the world of lepers, cripples, and prostitutes and *touched* them. The warmth of a human hand touching them at their point of deepest pain awakened within them a hope that had been all but lost, and, combined with their faith, it allowed healing to flow. The Divine touch restored their dignity and drew them back into the fold of humankind. Fear was dispelled and souls were refreshed. With the touch, doubt was dismantled and faith was discharged.

And He stretched out His hand and touched him, saying, "I am willing; be cleansed." And immediately his leprosy was cleansed (Matthew 8:3).

And He touched her hand, and the fever left her; and she arose, and waited on Him (Matthew 8:15).

Then He touched their eyes, saying, "Be it done to you according to your faith" (Matthew 9:29).

And Jesus came to them and touched them and said, "Arise, and do not be afraid" (Matthew 17:7).

And moved with compassion, Jesus touched their eyes; and immediately they regained their sight and followed Him (Matthew 20:34).

And moved with compassion, He stretched out His hand, and touched him, and said to him, "I am willing; be cleansed" (Mark 1:41).

And He came up and touched the coffin; and the bearers came to a halt. And He said, "Young man, I say to you, arise!" (Luke 7:14)

To the abiding rancor of the sanctimonious religious leaders, no self-preservative fear or religious inhibition prevented this Man from touching the *defiled*, as such were religiously defined. Lepers, prostitutes, blind, filthy, crippled, the poor, and even the dead—He reached out to them with moving compassion and gathered them to Himself. There, within His arms, they experienced the warmth of Heaven's love and received the healing and forgiveness they so craved.

Jesus violated every conceivable tradition when it came to His associations with the marginalized of Jewish society. He infuriated the Pharisees with every compassionate touch. The Qumran community of the Essenes had an unconditional law: "No madman, or lunatic, or simpleton, or fool, no blind man, or maimed, or lame, or deaf man, and no minor shall enter the community."[2]

Jesus came to shatter these man-made laws with the vengeance of Heaven. It was these very rejected ones whom He had come to save. To the Pharisees He declared, "But go and learn what this means, 'I desire compassion, and not sacrifice,' for I did not come to call the righteous, but sinners."[3] The Pharisees surrounded themselves with the rich, the wise, the educated, and the elite of society. Jesus, conversely, surrounded Himself with the poor, the uneducated, the rejected, and the outcasts of society.

---

2. Phillip Yancey, *The Jesus I Never Knew* (Grand Rapids, Michigan: Zondervan Publishing House, 1995), 153.

3. Matthew 9:13.

Loving compassion will draw all men.

This passionate devotion to the poor did not go unnoticed by the surrounding populace. They streamed to Him in ever-growing numbers...the broken, the sick, the helpless, sinners, lunatics, demon-possessed, common folk, prostitutes, rebels, the disinherited, and the dispossessed. Throughout His earthly ministry, He never could escape the crowds of people mesmerized by His kindness and irresistibly drawn to His tenderness. This Divine alliance of loving compassion and healing action drew the hopeful to Him day after day. There was no rest from the masses who desperately followed Him wherever He went—and His Shepherd's heart could not resist these poor, lost sheep.

On any given day you could find Him dining in places like the home of Simon the leper, or in the streets protecting a prostitute from the outraged attack of religious hypocrites, or walking the roadways in search of those who were lost and shunned by society.

They pressed in all around Him. If only they could touch Him. If only they could get His attention. All throughout the land they had heard of the power of His touch and longed to experience that human-Divine connection for themselves.

For she was saying to herself, "If I only touch His garment, I shall get well" (Matthew 9:21).

And they began to entreat Him that they might just touch the fringe of His cloak; and as many as touched it were cured (Matthew 14:36).

For He had healed many, with the result that all those who had afflictions pressed about Him in order to touch Him (Mark 3:10).

And wherever He entered villages, or cities, or countryside, they were laying the sick in the market places, and entreating Him that they might just touch the fringe of His cloak; and as many as touched it were being cured (Mark 6:56).

And they came to Bethsaida. And they brought a blind man to Him, and entreated Him to touch him (Mark 8:22).

And all the multitude were trying to touch Him, for power was coming from Him and healing them all (Luke 6:19).

Who is our neighbor?

One of the many parables Jesus taught was the Parable of the Good Samaritan. This story is rich in hidden subtleties and caustic innuendoes. In this one seemingly simple story Jesus touched on the issues of racial superiority, clerical disassociation, and social dysfunctionalism. Jesus chided the Pharisees for their blindness to the plight of the desperate humans all around them, embarrassed them with His reference to the Samaritan healer, and exposed their spiritual inconsistencies. Is not the heart of religion to reach out and bring help to those in need? Is it not to be more than simply religious services and communal practices? Does not our God expect us to reach beyond our own spiritual practices and religious abodes to embrace the rejected and bruised?

A lawyer initiated Jesus' telling of this parable with this question: "Who is my neighbor?"[4] Jesus made it very clear that the implications of "neighbor" extend to all who are in need. None should be stranded, or excluded, outside of the circle. That question still stands before the Church in our day. Who is our "neighbor"? Is he only the one whom we are comfortable with? Are we not to reach out and embrace the man with AIDS? Who will reach out to befriend the destitute found in our cities, if not us? Is there someone who will find a place for the homeless? Who will cross the line and embrace the "defiled" ones of our generation, if not those who have the Divine Life of the Father and the Son deposited within them? Where are those today who walk the streets of the destitute?

Paul tapped into that passion when he wrote under the inspiration of the Spirit,

> *But God chose the foolish things of the world to shame the wise; God chose the weak things of the world to shame the strong. He chose the lowly things of this world and the despised things—and the things that are not—to nullify the things that are* (1 Corinthians 1:27-28 NIV).

It was the eternal plan of Jesus, in His human form and in His heavenly body, to take the powerless and weak of the world and mold them into a community of grace that would overthrow the system of the evil one. If you look at every move of God down through the centuries, you will see the poor, the hurting, the weak, and the broken crowding around the message of the Savior. This always was and always will be the strength of

---

4.   Luke 10:29.

Christianity—unconditional love for the rejected and disenfranchised of the household of man.

Jesus expected that all who would be His disciples would also embrace His passion for the underprivileged. He frequently challenged those who sought to follow Him by confronting them with the issue of the poor. He would confront the rich, who relied on their possessions, and challenge them to give up all and share with the poor (thus qualifying them for the Kingdom of Heaven).

Jesus said to him, "If you wish to be complete, go and sell your possessions and give to the poor, and you shall have treasure in heaven; and come, follow Me" (Matthew 19:21).

And when Jesus heard this, He said to him, "One thing you still lack; sell all that you possess, and distribute it to the poor, and you shall have treasure in heaven; and come, follow Me" (Luke 18:22).

The burning fire of this passion of Jesus ignited the early Church and set the known world ablaze. Throughout the history of the early Church, the consistent love and care for the poor and those in need marked it as being of the Christ.

For there was not a needy person among them, for all who were owners of land or houses would sell them and bring the proceeds of the sales, and lay them at the apostles' feet; and they would be distributed to each, as any had need (Acts 4:34-35).

For Macedonia and Achaia have been pleased to make a contribution for the poor among the saints in Jerusalem (Romans 15:26).

After an intense debate on Gentile converts' observations of Jewish law, the apostles made this declaration to Paul and his companions, as he later related: "They only asked us to remember the poor—the very thing I also was eager to do."[5]

Tragically, this passion for the poor and needy steadily diminished as the Church turned inward. In an effort to resist the pressures of persecution and the horror of heresies, they began the construction of the *wall*. This *wall*, this barrier, continued to be built over time; it kept heresies out and protected the Church from persecution. This "catacomb" mentality of the Church finally settled into indifference toward the needs of men. Jesus made it clear that He did not want to take His followers out of the world;

5. Galatians 2:10.

He sent them into the world to be ambassadors of Heaven. But by the second century this passion had all but disappeared from the Church.

There have been those, however, who down through the centuries rediscovered this same heartfelt empathy of Jesus for the plight of humanity. What were their testimonies like?

Compassion is restored throughout the ages.

One of the first followers of the Lord to rediscover the Lord's passion for the poor was St. Francis of Assisi. He was born in 1182, the son of one of the most well-to-do families in Assisi. Occasional incidents in his younger days revealed some intolerance in his heart, but it was on one of those occasions that the seed of his future transformation was planted. One day while working intently in his father's cloth shop arranging the fabric, a beggar came to the door and asked for alms in God's name. Francis rudely kicked the man out, but at once he regretted his actions and followed the man to offer his apologies. This event replayed in his mind over and over again.

Later on in his life, during a brief stay in Rome, he took out his money, took off his garments, and gave them all to the poor. On another occasion he encountered a leper in Assisi and, instead of fleeing as most villagers did, he went up to him and embraced him. He did all this despite the scorn of his friends and his father's great disappointment. His steps before him were ordered; that leper represented Christ Himself! So Francis renounced his father's possessions and went on to work among the poor and leprous people of his time.

Here are the oft-quoted words of St. Francis:

> Lord, make me an instrument of Thy peace;
> Where there is hatred, let me sow charity;
> Where there is injury, pardon;
> Where there is error, the truth;
> Where there is doubt, the faith;
> Where there is despair, hope;
> Where there is darkness, light; and
> Where there is sadness, joy.
> O, Divine Master,
> Grant that I may not so much seek to be consoled, as to console;
> To be understood as to understand;
> To be loved as to love;

> For it is in giving that we receive;
> It is in pardoning that we are pardoned.

As noted earlier, Madame Guyon was one of the most outstanding spiritual writers of the 1600s. She was known for her deep spiritual perception and for her pursuit of union with God. Besides her spiritual writings, she also was known for her compassion for the poor and deprived. Read her own words from her autobiography:

> "In acts of charity I was assiduous. So great was my tenderness for the poor, that I wished to supply all their wants. I could not see their necessity, without reproaching myself for the plenty I enjoyed. I deprived myself of all I could to help them. The best at my table was distributed among them. Being refused by others, they all came to me.

> "God used me to reclaim several from their disorderly lives. I went to visit the sick, to comfort them, to make their beds. I made ointments, dressed their wounds, buried their dead. I furnished tradesmen and mechanics wherewith to keep their shops. My heart was much opened toward my fellow-creatures in distress."[6]

In the late 1600s and 1700s the Pietistic Movement swept across Eastern Europe and eventually touched the eastern shores of North America. This was a reform movement predominantly within the Lutheran church. One of its central figures, August Francke, insisted that they place greater value on a "drop of true love more than a sea of knowledge." On the foundation of this movement the Quakers in the 1800s caught the passion of Jesus for the poor and the marginalized of society. They insisted that the quiet inward life become inevitably associated with its active outward expression in the world of affairs. And so it was.

Elizabeth Fry rose above her own natural fears and invaded the women's section of the Newgate Prison in London in the early 1800s. She succeeded in changing the lives of the "savage, and drunken, unruly women."[7]

The Quakers were the first to reach out to the mentally ill. Instead of treating them as animals, they established a retreat for them. There these

---

6. Abbie C. Morrow, ed. *Sweet Smelling Myrrh* (Salem, Ohio: Schmul Publishing, 1996), 65,66.

7. Donald Durnbaugh, *The Believer's Church* (New York: The Macmillan Company, 1968), 273.

compassionate people treated them as guests and removed the typical physical restraints.[8]

Quakers also took a strong stand against slavery. As early as the late 1600s they were lifting their voice up against the degradation of human slavery.

> "Woolman would often decline to accept hospitality in a home where slaves were kept or would insist upon reimbursing slaves for work done for him personally....A Mennonite, Peter Plockhoy, issued the first public statement in North America against slavery in connection with regulations for a colony on the Delaware: 'No lordships or servile slavery shall burden our company.' "[9]

One of the great lights of social reform in the chronicles of history is the British statesman William Wilberforce. Wilberforce would become the key political leader in the abolition of the slave trade. He was a tiny "shrimp" of a man, but he was gigantic in his courage and tenacious in his struggle against a very popular trade. It was a cause that he believed in and to which he dedicated all of his adult life.

William was strongly influenced in his early life by his aunt and uncle who were very much involved in Methodism. He would later declare to his mother that George Whitefield had put something of a fire in his heart that would remain forever. The Methodist had taught him the importance of getting involved in a cause larger than oneself.

For William the cause would be to forever remove the blight of slavery from the face of British history. The fight would be long and arduous, demanding every ounce of energy his soul possessed. There would be times of failure and deep depression when it seemed that he would never win this war. John Newton, the redeemed ex-slave trader, would be a source of tremendous encouragement for Wilberforce in those times of discouragement.

On the fateful day of February 23, 1807, Wilberforce stepped into the Parliamentary House knowing that this was the day. For more than 40 years William had led the charge against the slave trade. This day would be the climax of a life's work. Sir Andrew Romilly stood up to address the House. Every eye was upon him. In referring to the conquests of Napoleon at that time, he would begin:

---

8.   Durnbaugh, *The Believer's Church*, 274.
9.   Durnbaugh, *The Believer's Church*, 275.

" 'And when I compare...those pangs of remorse,' continued Romilly, 'with the feelings of which must accompany my honorable friend [speaking of Wilberforce] from this House to his home, after the vote tonight shall have confirmed the object of his human and unceasing labors; when he retires...to his happy and delightful family, when he lays himself down on his bed, reflecting on the innumerable voices that will be raised in every quarter of the world to bless him, how much more pure and perfect felicity must he enjoy, in the consciousness of having preserved so many millions of his fellow creatures, than—' "[10]

Romilly could not finish the speech because the whole House erupted in an ovation of honor for Wilberforce.

At the end of the day the House passed by a vote of 283 to 6 to abolish the slave trade.

From his deathbed, John Wesley wrote concerning Wilberforce, "I see not how you can go through your glorious enterprise in opposing that execrable villainy, which is the scandal of religion, of England, and of human nature. Unless God has raised you up for this very thing, you will be worn out by the opposition of men and devils. But if God be for you, who can be against you?"[11]

John Wesley himself was one of the first to move outside the confines of the church building and reach out to the poor and destitute. He made this entry in his Journal on Saturday, March 31:

"In the evening I reached Bristol, and met Mr. Whitefield there. I could scarce reconcile myself at first to this strange way of preaching in the fields, of which he set me an example on Sunday; having been all my life (until very lately) so tenacious of every point relating to decency and order, that I should have thought of souls almost a sin if it had not been done in a church."[12]

John Wesley was actively involved in reaching out to the unemployed. In fact, at the age of 82 he spent whole days walking about to collect money

---

10. Charles Ludwig, *He Freed Britian's Slaves* (Scottdale, Pennsylvania: Herald Press, 1977), 188.

11. *Christian History Magazine*, Vol. XVI, No. 1, 1997, p. 12.

12. Howard Snyder, *The Radical Wesley* (Downers Grove, Illinois: InterVarsity Press, 1980), 33.

for the poor. George Whitefield, the man who introduced Wesley to field preaching among the poor, maintained an orphanage for the abandoned in the state of Georgia.

Moving into the 1900s, we have many examples of people who abandoned the luxuries of a capitalistic society to embrace the needy of the Third World. No one else stands out more than the late Mother Teresa.

She was born Agnes Gonxha Bojaxhiu in 1910 in Skopje, Yugoslavia (now Macedonia). In 1928 she decided to become a nun and went to Dublin, Ireland, to join the Sisters of Loreto. From there she went to the Loreto convent in Darjeeling, India.

In 1929 she began to teach geography at St. Mary's High School for Girls in Calcutta. In those days the streets of Calcutta were crowded with beggars, lepers, and the homeless. Unwanted infants were regularly abandoned on the streets or in garbage bins. In 1946, Mother Teresa felt the need to abandon her teaching position to care for the needy in the slums of Calcutta.

Initially focusing her efforts on poor children in the streets, Mother Teresa taught them how to read and how to care for themselves. Many former students of St. Mary's eventually joined her order. Each girl who joined was required to devote her life to serving the poor without accepting any material reward in return.

In the mid-1950s, Mother Teresa added aid to lepers in her work. The Indian government gave her order 34 acres near the city of Asansol. There she established a leper colony, called Shanti Nagar (Town of Peace). Within a few years her work expanded beyond India, and the Sisters of Charity opened centers throughout the world for lepers, the blind, the disabled, the aged, and the dying, as well as schools and orphanages for the poor.

The recipient of various awards, including the Nobel Peace Prize, Mother Teresa used all the money that accompanied those awards to fund her centers. By 1990 more than 3,000 nuns belonged to the Missionaries of Charity, operating various centers in 25 different countries.[13]

F.B. Meyer, a Baptist minister, exemplified what welfare at the local church level can do. While at Melbourne Hall, Leicester, in the 1880s, Meyer combined evangelism with social programs. Some of his main thrusts were rehabilitating ex-prisoners and helping people whose lives were

---

13.   Mother Theresa. January 22, 1997. October 8, 1999. <http://www.nalejandria.com/
      utopia/english/MotherTheresa-eng.htm/>.

being ruined by alcohol. Meyer saw alcohol as the typical cause of crime, but he soon discovered what a difficult time men coming out of prison had in finding jobs. So he set up businesses to employ these men. "F.B. Meyer —Firewood Merchant" is only one example.[14]

There are a few illustrations in this present time of those who have maintained the Lord's passion for the poor. The YWAM Mercy ships go from port to port throughout the world delivering medical help and food for the poor. The Salvation Army continues to give food and relief to those in the inner cities around the world. Teen Challenge centers have reached out to those whose lives have been destroyed by drugs, alcohol, and other addictions. There are some city churches that have not abandoned the inner city, but have remained there as a source of relief and strength to those fighting the battle of poverty, unemployment, and crime.

In spite of these few examples of Christian concern for the poor, the advance of technology in our generation has served only to increase the gap between the confines of the Church and the need in the streets. We preach gospel messages from our safe TV studios to the faceless masses of our nation. We post our "message of hope and concern" over the lines of the Internet, hoping that some lost soul will be "touched." Now there's an unusual word to use in this American culture of technological evangelism. This is not the same "touch" that we saw in the life of the Master. Can a cyber-touch alleviate the pain and heartache of those trapped in poverty, addictions, and hopeless loneliness?

We nestle down in the comfortable pews of our richly constructed church buildings where we enjoy the security of a safe environment. There we pray for the poor and needy ones in our community. Our prayers are quite fervent, but our actions are anemic. The time has come to break out of our comfortable buildings and places of refuge to once again engage ourselves in the world for whom our Master gave up all the "comfort" and glory of His heavenly dwelling to seek and to save.

May the Lord restore the *touch* of compassion and power in this day!

---

14.   Ian Randall, "Evangelicals and Social Reform," *The Care Review* (December 1997; Vol. 9, Issue 2). October 8, 1999. <http://www.care.org.uk/issues/ls/ ls971201.htm/>.

Chapter 8

Part I

The Passion for the Divine Presence

JOHN 17:5 SAYS, "And now, glorify Thou Me together with Thyself, Father, with the glory which I had with Thee before the world was."

Jehovah's intervention in the beginning days of Israel's history was motivated by His sympathy for the poor and by Israel's oppressive conditions in the land of Egypt. Their cry for deliverance pierced through the gates of Heaven and moved the heart of their seemingly elusive and enigmatic God. This God responded, however, and Israel soon had her first encounter with the Divine Presence. First, though, her leader needed to have his own date with destiny. There at the foot of Mount Horeb, God gave Moses a brief, fleeting glimpse of His Glory. The allure of the burning bush led him into the "place of meeting" where Heaven and earth converged. The Voice of God quickly overwhelmed Moses' initial intrigue and wonder with the burning bush, and Moses found himself engaged in a bewildering dialogue with the Elohim of Israel. He was given his Divine commission there at that holy meeting place. It was his first encounter with the Glory.

Israel is introduced to the Glory.

M oses, an aging shepherd, was to return to the rich and powerful captor nation of the Israelites and, with a shepherd's rod, lead these chosen people out of captivity and into the land of promise. His only source of strength and comfort would be the Presence of Yahweh.

Moses would eventually lead the people back to this very mountain for their own rendezvous with the glorious Presence of Yahweh. Israel would be conceived in this Glory. It was the Divine Presence (Glory) hovering over Israel that distinguished her as a nation. It is this Presence that gives birth to a people and sets them apart for Divine purpose. The promise to Moses of God's continuing Presence would be Israel's solace and strength as she crossed the Jordan and established herself in the land of Canaan.

> "As they move through an economic wilderness, the liberated slaves cannot develop into a coherent community unless they are converted into priestly agents for the Sovereign of history. The Horeb theophany is to transform the uncouth mass of slaves into a united people of free men and women. Presence, after the fire is extinct and the thunders are silent, will transmute its shattering but momentary impact into a sociological cement which will create a sacerdotal realm, thus a holy nation."[1]

All of Israel's great kings and prophets had their own unique visitations with the Presence. David battled the enemies of Israel while safeguarded by the shield of Glory. Under the inspirational and reflective light of that Glory he composed many of the great psalms of Israel. The Divine passion burned within him; he desired a continual habitation within the realm of rapturous Glory.

> *But Thou, O Lord, art a shield about me, my glory, and the One who lifts my head* (Psalm 3:3).

> *O Lord, I love the habitation of Thy house, and the place where Thy glory dwells* (Psalm 26:8).

Solomon had built the great temple and watched in awe as the Glory of God descended and filled it, sanctifying it for priestly function. "Now when Solomon had finished praying, fire came down from heaven and

---

1.   Samuel Terrien, *The Elusive Presence* (New York: Harper & Row, 1978), 124.

consumed the burnt offering and the sacrifices; and the glory of the Lord filled the house."[2]

One by one the renowned prophets of Israel, under the unction of the Spirit, spoke of the coming Glory of God. They envisioned a day when the Glory would move from singular encounters with man toward societal exhibitions to the whole world.

> *Then the Lord will create over the whole area of Mount Zion and over her assemblies a cloud by day, even smoke, and the brightness of a flaming fire by night; for over all the glory will be a canopy* (Isaiah 4:5).

> *Then the glory of the Lord will be revealed, and all flesh will see it together; for the mouth of the Lord has spoken* (Isaiah 40:5).

> *And behold, the glory of the God of Israel was coming from the way of the east. And His voice was like the sound of many waters; and the earth shone with His glory* (Ezekiel 43:2).

> *For the earth will be filled with the knowledge of the glory of the Lord, as the waters cover the sea* (Habakkuk 2:14).

> *"For I,"* declares the Lord, *"will be a wall of fire around her, and I will be the glory in her midst"* (Zechariah 2:5).

The early kings of ancient Israel reigned in the sunshine of its Divine brilliance and the prophets of old prophesied of its dazzling splendor. The Glory was the poetic inspiration of the psalmists, enabling this celebrated music guild to write majestic expressions to the One God. It was the Glory that distinguished little Israel as a nation amongst the community of nations in those early days.

Ichabod: The Glory departs.

Jilted by Israel's idolatry and immorality, the Glory of God lifted and left Israel in the same bondage in which the Divine Presence had found her so many years before. No longer was the Glory of God her protective panoply or her majestic sanctuary. Ezekiel the prophet watched in pain as the Glory departed, and he penned those ignominious words, *ichabod*: "the Glory has departed"!

For too long the Glory had been painfully absent. It remained only a faint memory even for the most spiritually attuned in Israel. The warmth of that heavenly brilliance had been exchanged for the chill of imperial slavery.

---

2.   2 Chronicles 7:1.

Having lived under the dominion of one nation after another, Israel now lived under the shadow of the mighty dissolute Caesars of Rome.

Left alone without the security of the Presence, the children of Israel's only comfort was found in the collection of historical books that recorded the history of the ancient Glory. The only "song" they had were the songs written during the glorious reign of David. These songs served to remind them that the once present Glory of Yahweh had faded. Strangely enough, the songs of the poets and the statements of the prophets stirred only a few. Only a small remnant longed for a fresh dramatic display of Yahweh's Presence.

In an attempt to resurrect the ancient Glory, Herod determined to rebuild the temple. It would not be Solomon's temple; nevertheless, Herod was able to create a pageantry type of worship and a physical similitude of that former temple. With the construction of his temple came a fresh resurgence of religious activity. The daily sacrifices again spread their aroma throughout Jerusalem. The city became alive with the scurry of priests rushing to fulfill their important religious duties and with the clamor of businessmen taking material advantage of this newly revived religious fervor. The sound of musical instruments could be heard even to the far corners of the city. Descendants of Abraham, Isaac, and Jacob traveled to the temple hoping for, at the least, a simple brush with the Eternal One. They longed to see and experience the Presence, the God of their forefathers.

Herod did his best to restore the illustrious days of Solomon. But something was woefully missing. In spite of the spiritual burst of ecclesiastical performance and resurrected religion, a melancholy pervaded the temple. A lethargic loneliness could be felt in the many courts and rooms of this man-made "dwelling place for God." Everyone was in his place and performing his task, but something that could not be defined was strikingly missing. As the high priest entered into the Holy of Holies enshrouded in a cloud of incense, it was...*almost* like the days of old except for one "small thing": *The Presence of Yahweh was not in there!* That awesome Divine Presence of Glory was not to be found in that room. He was not in any of the rooms. He was not in the house. He was not to be found at the gates. Nor was He found in the city. He was not to be found anywhere in the nation of Israel. They had built their temple, but they had not brought back the Glory! God had chosen not to live in the house that they had built for Him.

The Glory of God is localized in a Man.

From the effulgent radiant heights of His Father's Glory, Jesus descended into the empty ritualism that characterized man's vain attempt to reproduce the Glory. John chapter 1 declares that the Eternal Logos became flesh and pitched His tent with man. Some gazed, face forward, into His Glory—the Glory that traveled with Him from the Presence of His Father. Encompassed within that Glory, He was conceived by the Spirit in the womb of Mary.

> *And the angel answered and said to her, "The Holy Spirit will come upon you, and the power of the Most High will overshadow you; and for that reason the holy offspring shall be called the Son of God"* (Luke 1:35).

The word *overshadow* that Luke used to describe the procreation of Jesus is the same Greek word that the Septuagint uses to describe the Glory of God over the tabernacle in the Book of Exodus.[3] The Glory of God had been manifested to Moses in a burning bush and to Israel in the dark thunderous clouds over Mount Sinai. Its transcendent brightness had filled the temple and been set in prophetic exhibition before the prophets of old. But this time the Glory overshadows a young Jewish maiden, preparing her to bring forth God's Son into the world.

The Glory of God had never been fully manifested in a man. Now it will find a place of habitation in the Son of Man.

The backside of God's Glory is unveiled in His goodness to man.

> *This beginning of His signs Jesus did in Cana of Galilee, and manifested His glory, and His disciples believed in Him* (John 2:11).

> *But when Jesus heard it, He said, "This sickness is not unto death, but for the glory of God, that the Son of God may be glorified by it"* (John 11:4).

Jesus had embodied the manifested Presence of His Father's Glory. It was His great passion to release that Glory on the poor, the sick, and the destitute of humankind. With unbelievable restraint He patiently waited for the time appointed by His Father. There would be no shortcuts and no premature presentations of Father's Glory.

When the time was perfect, He removed the humble cloak of anonymity and let the light of the Glory within be visibly manifested in His kindness and goodness toward men. The Glory was revealed in an unprecedented demonstration of power over the works of darkness. No longer did it symbolize death to those who crossed the line, mishandled the ark, or

---

3.   See Exodus 40:35.

entered His Presence unprepared. The Glory became a source of life and healing for all who reached out in faith. The Glory left an abundance of goodness and mercy in its wake. God's never-ending love toward man could be seen in that trail of Glory.

The Glory was back! What Herod's temple lacked, was now made manifest in the earthly ministry of Jesus. The backside of the Glory of God was unveiled in His goodness to man. Moses entreated God to reveal His Glory, but the request was denied. Instead, God allowed Moses to see the backside of His Glory as He exposed His goodness to him. Is it possible that Moses was given a premiere showing of the future, incarnate work of God's Son?

Nevertheless, the Glory remained elusive to many. Their fascination with the miraculous blinded them to the real miracle! They seemed oblivious to the Divine Presence that dwelt within this extraordinary Man. The Glory was right in their midst, but they were unable to detect its presence.

"The fullness of the divine reality was present in a peculiar hiddenness. The glory was not superimposed upon the carnal finitude. The body of a historical man was not a window through which the glory could be glimpsed. It was the body itself which at once concealed and revealed the glory."[4]

Only those who were closest to Him were able to penetrate the hidden quality of the elusive Presence. Through the power of faith they were able to transcend their own earthly finiteness and peek into the true nature of their Master and friend.

With great passion the Lord desired to reveal the divine Glory of His Father. It had too long been shrouded in mystery. But the Glory has a peculiar quality about it, for it is a true paradox. The Glory is powerful, majestic, and overwhelming; yet, it is enigmatic, veiled, and mysterious. It is discerningly visible only to the one who has faith. Faith finds a way to solve the mystery of the Glory's hiddenness and awaken the power of its magnificent grandeur. Because the Master passionately desired to have men experience its energy, He sought out those of faith.

---

4.   Terrien, *The Elusive Presence*, 421.

Yahweh manifests His Presence
on the mountain for a second time.

And six days later, Jesus took with Him Peter and James and John, and brought them up to a high mountain by themselves. And He was transfigured before them (Mark 9:2).

And the glory of the Lord rested on Mount Sinai, and the cloud covered it for six days; and on the seventh day He called to Moses from the midst of the cloud (Exodus 24:16).

One cannot but be intrigued by the similarities between these two events. Both have the cloud that envelops the mountain, an aura of anticipation, and the Presence of God manifested by the dramatic Voice that speaks out of the cloud.

Moses had been once denied the vision of the front side of the Glory, but on *this* mountain—along with these dazed disciples—he finally and supernaturally received the answer to his prayer. The Glory of God found a way to express itself to man in a fully orbed manifestation of the Divine Light of the full nature of Almighty God.

And He was transfigured before them; and His face shone like the sun, and His garments became as white as light (Matthew 17:2).

Matthew uses the Greek verb *metamorphoo* to describe the drama that unfolded before the eyes of the three disciples. The Glory was under "house arrest" in the body of Jesus; but once the restraining order was lifted, there was a resplendent exhibition of the mysterious Glory of God. In Philippians 2 Paul says that Jesus existed in the form of God, but that somewhere in His descent toward earth He took on the humble form of a bond-servant. There on the mountain Jesus allowed that community of three to see His real essence...who He really was! The Divine nature had never left Him; instead, it had been masked by the form of human flesh.

He had waited for this moment with great patience and expectancy. He had spoken of His Divine nature with parabolic language while all the while longing to show His true self to His disciples. Under the Father's direction, He carefully selected the three who would be privileged participants in this cosmic event. John described it this way: "And the Word became flesh, and dwelt among us, and we beheld His glory,

glory as of the only begotten from the Father, full of grace and truth."[5]

The shining brilliance of the Glory changed the very similitude of Jesus. His face blazed with the luminescence of Divine Presence and His clothes with the luster of Divine Energy. He regally stood before them in open disclosure of His eternal, veritable nature. He dipped, however briefly, into eternity and enjoyed, for a few precious moments, that preexistent, eternal communion of glorious honor that belonged to Him as the only begotten of the Father.

In the midst of this spectacular display of heavenly glory, Luke recorded that Elijah and Moses were discussing with Jesus His coming suffering in Jerusalem.[6] What a strange discussion! In the midst of Heaven's Glory they speak of the coming dark days of suffering. They, no doubt, spoke of the betrayal and the intrigue that would surround those days. In this conversation we are reminded that the goal of reaching ultimate Glory always leads down the path of human suffering. If one avoids the suffering, he will miss the Glory! Remember Paul's words in Romans 8:17-18:

...if indeed we suffer with Him in order that we may also be glorified with Him. For I consider that the sufferings of this present time are not worthy to be compared with the glory that is to be revealed to us.

This morbid discussion of the cross in no way diminished the wonder of this breathtaking and wholly extraordinary event. Nevertheless, it did lend an element of soberness to this amazing and memorable moment.

The disciples had been on the sidelines, as it were, as simple, awestruck spectators. But when the dramatic exhibition of shimmering Glory came to its conclusion, Peter had to speak. Overwhelmed by his exposure to the glorious Presence, Peter fumbled around in search of words that expressed his awe. In the ecstasy of the moment, his trembling voice suggested that they build a memorial.

We tend to be hard on Peter for his impetuous human reaction to this stunning encounter with the "transfigured Christ." Yet throughout history mortals have been tempted to either erect structures that solemnize a visitation with God or turn those events into nostalgic contemplation that prevent them from going on to fresh experiences with the Glory. Unfortunately, these attempts to hallow those moments for posterity's sake usually produce

---

5.   John 1:14.

6.   See Luke 9:31.

shrines that imprison man in past experiences. Clinging to the past always limits fresh encounters with the Glory.

The Glory of God prepares the way for the Voice of God.

As on Mount Sinai, a cloud dramatically spreads itself over the mountaintop even as Peter still speaks. The disciples are enveloped in the cloud and are confronted by the Voice of the unseen God. Every encounter with the Glory of God leads to a word from God. The Glory of God creates a pathway for His Voice. The Glory of God arrests our attention so that we are attuned to the Voice.

The Voice of God thunderously delivers a command to hear the Son. God does not escort man into His glorious Presence for mere theatrical displays of power to titillate his senses and satisfy his curiosity. Man descends the "mountain of glory" with a word that must be obeyed. Glory is always linked to the Voice! From the midst of His infinite Glory, the Eternal God speaks His will. The Glory of God is manifested as the Word of God: "And the Word became flesh, and dwelt among us, and we beheld His glory...."[7] It is the manifestation of the Word that gives presence to the Glory.

Man will be tempted to linger in Glory's rapturous afterglow. The fascination with Divine manifestations is irresistible but dangerous, if it means we miss the Voice. Whether God chooses to manifest His Glory in a burning bush, in a dark cloud, or even through a mortal man, we must be careful that our eyes do not so fully focus on the manifestations that our spiritual ears do not hear the Voice that speaks and brings revelation of the Divine purposes.

It was in the eternal glory of union before the beginning of time that the Voice of God spoke, "Who will go for Us?" In loving and joyful submission to the will of the Supreme One, the Son accepted the mission. In John 17:4-5 He pronounced:

> *I glorified Thee on the earth, having accomplished the work which Thou hast given Me to do. And now, glorify Thou Me together with Thyself, Father, with the glory which I had with Thee before the world was.*

The finished work of Christ resulted in an ever-increasing expansion of the Glory on the earth. The Glory of Heaven was manifested on earth by the Son's abandoning Himself to the Divine Will and to His accomplishing the Divine Work. His ultimate passion was to bring glory to the

---

7.   John 1:14.

Father. He rejected the glory of man and pursued the honor and Glory of the Almighty God. He laid down a spiritual principle for all time: He who pursues the glory of man does not participate in the Glory of the Father. He who rejects the glory of man is rewarded with the Glory of the Father.

Man is invited into the intimate place of Glory.

And the glory which Thou hast given Me I have given to them; that they may be one, just as We are one (John 17:22).

Father, I desire that they also, whom Thou hast given Me, be with Me where I am, in order that they may behold My glory, which Thou hast given Me; for Thou didst love Me before the foundation of the world (John 17:24).

The Glory is a place of intimacy and union. It was Jesus' great abiding passion that His followers become part of that intimate circle that encompasses the glorious Oneness of the eternal God. Jesus' heart cry to His Father was that the created being, man, would be included in the fraternity of the heavenly Glory.

By perfectly completing the Father's mission, Jesus made a way for man to be liberated from the dark, hopeless dungeon of sin's oppression and to be incorporated into the circle of Father's Presence.

The earthly task was successfully concluded. The veil of separation was rent. A gateway was opened that permitted man to move from being a mere spectator of the Glory to becoming a container of the Glory.

The transfer is complete and the next task begins. Mortal man will now be prepared to become the new expression of the Glory of God on the earth. It was Jesus' great passion that His disciples of all generations experience the dynamic of that Glory. The apostle Paul picked up on that theme and, by revelation, declared that through the path of suffering the child of God is able to enter into that dimension of Glory. "If indeed we suffer with Him in order that we may also be glorified with Him."[8]

As we will see in Part II, John Flavel captured that same theme in his writing on the Glory of Christ when he wrote, "The angels will admire the beauty and glory of the spouse of Christ."

---

8.   Romans 8:17b.

Chapter 8

Part II

Christic Altogether Lovely[1]

*John Flavel was born in Worcestershire, England, and was a contemporary of Madame Guyon. He was extremely diligent in his studies and exceeded many of his peers in university. He eventually ended up at Dartmouth where he pastored for most of his life. Much like Madame Guyon, he also experienced many hardships. Nevertheless, he applied himself to continual study of the Scriptures, was very gifted in prayer, and was thoroughly devoted to his precious flock in Dartmouth. His writings reflected his passion for the Lord Jesus. His text, **Christ Altogether Lovely**, was never published, but it was a true example of that passion.*

Flavel describes with affection and artistic eloquence the glory as it is expressed in the Person of the Lord Jesus. There is nothing that can compare to the glory of the "Word made flesh." Concerning this Jesus he writes, "God never presented to the world such a vision of glory before."

*   *   *

1.   John Flavel, *Christ Altogether Lovely*. May 27, 1999. October 8, 1999. <http://www.ccel.org/f/flavel/lovely/lovely.html/>. Public domain. Reprinted as is.

John Flavel

CHRIST IS TO BE LOVED.

"Yes, He is altogether lovely." Song of Songs 5:16.

At the ninth verse of this chapter, you have a question put forth by the daughters of Jerusalem, "What is your beloved more than another beloved?" The spouse answers, "He is the chief among ten thousand." She then recounts many of the things she finds so excellent in her beloved and then concludes with these words that I have read: "Yes, he is altogether lovely."

The words set forth the transcendent loveliness of the Lord Jesus Christ, and naturally resolve themselves into three parts:

1. Who he is.
2. What he is.
3. What he is like.

First, *Who he is*: the Lord Jesus Christ, after whom she had been seeking, for whom she was overcome by love; concerning whom these daughters of Jerusalem had enquired: whom she had struggled to describe in his particular excellencies. He is the great and excellent subject of whom she here speaks.

Secondly, *What he is*, or what she claims of him: That he is a lovely one. The Hebrew word, which is often translated "desires," means "to earnestly desire, covet, or long after that which is most pleasant, graceful, delectable and admirable." The original word is both in the abstract, and plural in number, which says that Christ is the very essence of all delights and pleasures, the very soul and substance of them. As all the rivers are gathered into the ocean, which is the meeting-place of all the waters in the world, so Christ is that ocean in which all true delights and pleasures meet.

Thirdly, *What he is like*: He is altogether lovely, the every part to be desired. He is lovely when taken together, and in every part; as if she had said, "Look on him in what respect or particular you wish; cast your eye upon this lovely object, and view him any way, turn him in your serious thoughts which way you wish; consider his person, his offices, his works, or any other thing belonging to him; you will find him altogether lovely, There is nothing dis-agreeable in him, there is nothing lovely without him." Hence note,

DOCTRINE: That Jesus Christ is the loveliest person souls can set their eyes upon:

"Thou art fairer than the children of men." Psalm 14:2.

He is "Altogether Lovely"

Here it is said of Jesus Christ, which cannot be said of any mere creature, that he is "altogether lovely." In opening this point I shall,

1. Examine the importance of this phrase "altogether lovely."
2. Show you in what respect Christ is so.

WHAT IS MEANT BY "ALTOGETHER LOVELY"

Let us consider this excellent expression, and particularly reflect on what is contained in it, and you shall find this expression "altogether lovely."

First, *It excludes all unloveliness and disagreeableness from Jesus Christ.* As a theologian long ago said, "There is nothing in him which is not loveable." The excellencies of Jesus Christ are perfectly exclusive of all their opposites; there is nothing of a contrary property or quality found in him to contaminate or devaluate his excellency. And in this respect Christ infinitely transcends the most excellent and loveliest of created things. Whatsoever loveliness is found in them, it is not without a bad aftertaste. The fairest pictures must have their shadows: The rarest and most brilliant gems must have dark backgrounds to set off their beauty; the best creature is but a bitter sweet at best: If there is something pleasing, there is also something sour. if a person has every ability, both innate and acquired, to delight us, yet there is also some natural corruption intermixed with it to put us off. But it is not so in our altogether lovely Christ, his excellencies are pure and unmixed. He is a sea of sweetness without one drop of gall.

Secondly, "Altogether lovely," i.e. *There is nothing unlovely found in him,* so all that is in him is wholly lovely. As every ray of God is precious, so every thing that is in Christ is precious: Who can weigh Christ in a pair of balances, and tell you what his worth is? "His price is above rubies, and all that thou canst desire is not to be compared with him," Prov. 8:11.

Thirdly "Altogether lovely," i.e. *He embraces all things that are lovely*: he seals up the sum of all loveliness. Things that shine as single stars with a particular glory, all meet in Christ as a glorious constellation. Col. 1:19, "It pleased the Father that in him should all fullness dwell." Cast your eyes among all created beings, survey the universe: you will observe strength in one, beauty in a second, faithfulness in a third, wisdom in a fourth; but you shall find none excelling in them all as Christ does. Bread has one quality, water another, raiment another, medicine another; but none has them all in itself as Christ does. He is bread to the hungry, water to the thirsty, a garment to the naked, healing to the wounded; and whatever a soul can desire is found in him, 1 Cor. 1:30.

Fourthly, "Altogether lovely," i.e. *Nothing is lovely in opposition to him, or in separation from him*. If he truly is altogether lovely, then whatsoever is opposite to him, or separate from him can have no loveliness in it. Take away Christ, and where is the loveliness of any enjoyment? The best creature-comfort apart from Christ is but a broken cistern. It cannot hold one drop of true comfort, Psalm 73:26. It is with the creature—the sweetest and loveliest creature—as with a beautiful image in the mirror: turn away the face and where is the image? Riches, honours, and comfortable relations are sweet when the face of Christ smiles upon us through them; but without him, what empty trifles are they all?

Fifthly, "Altogether lovely," i.e. *Transcending all created excellencies in beauty and loveliness*. If you compare Christ and other things, no matter how lovely, no matter how excellent and desirable, Christ carries away all loveliness from them. "He is (as the apostle says) before all things," Col. 1:17. Not only before all things in time, nature, and order; but before all things in dignity, glory, and true excellence. In all things he must have the pre-eminence. Let us but compare Christ's excellence with the creature's in a few particulars, and how manifest will the transcendent loveliness of Jesus Christ appear! For,

1. All other loveliness is derived and secondary; but the loveliness of Christ is original and primary. Angels and men, the world and all the desirable things in it, receive what excellence they crave from him. They are streams from the fountain. The farther any thing departs from its fountain and original, the less excellency there is in it.

2. The loveliness and excellency of all other things, is only relative, consisting in its reference to Christ, and subservience to his glory. But Christ is lovely, considered absolutely in himself. He is desirable for himself; other things are desirable because of him.

3. The beauty and loveliness of all other things are fading and perishing; but the loveliness of Christ is fresh for all eternity. The sweetness of the best created thing is a fading flower; if not before, yet certainly at death it must fade away. Job 4:21. "Doth not their excellency, which is in them, go away?" Yes, yes, whether they are the natural excellencies of the body, acquired endowments of the mind, lovely features, graceful qualities, or anything else we find attractive; all these like pleasant flowers are withered, faded, and destroyed by death. "But Christ is still the same, yesterday, today, and for ever," Heb. 13:8.

4. The beauty and holiness of creatures are ensnaring and dangerous. A man may make an idol out of them, and indulge himself beyond the bounds of moderation with them, but there is no danger of excess in the love of Christ. The

soul is then in the healthiest frame and temper when it is most overwhelmed by love to Christ, Song of Songs 5:8.

5. The loveliness of every creature is of a confining and obstructing nature. Our esteem of it diminishes the closer we approach to it, or the longer we enjoy it. Creatures, like pictures, are fairest at a certain distance, but it is not so with Christ; the nearer the soul approaches him, and the longer it lives in the enjoyment of him, still the sweeter and more desirable he becomes.

6. All other loveliness cannot satisfy the soul of man. There is not scope enough in any one created thing, or in all the natural universe of created things for the soul of man to reach out and expand; but the soul still feels itself confined and narrowed within those limits. This comes to pass from the inadequacy and unsuitableness of the creature to the nobler and more excellent soul of man. The soul is like a ship in a narrow river which does not have room to turn. It is always running aground and foundering in the shallows. But Jesus Christ is in every way sufficient to the vast desires of the soul; in him it has sea-room enough. In him the soul may spread all its sails with no fear of touching bottom. And thus you see what is the importance of this phrase, "Altogether lovely."

HOW CHRIST IS "ALTOGETHER LOVELY"

Secondly, Next I promised to show you in what respects Jesus Christ is altogether lovely:

He is Lovely in His Person

First, He is altogether lovely in his person: he is Deity dwelling in flesh, John 1:14. The wonderful, perfect union of the divine and human nature in Christ renders him an object of admiration and adoration to both angels and men, 1 Tim. 3:16. God never presented to the world such a vision of glory before. Consider how the human nature of our Lord Jesus Christ is overflowing with all the graces of the Spirit, in such a way as never any of the saints was filled. O what a lovely picture does this paint of him! John 3:34, "God gives the Spirit [to him] without limit." This makes him "the most excellent of men and [his] lips have been anointed with grace," Psalm 45:2. If a small measure of grace in the saints makes them sweet and desirable companions, what must the riches of the Spirit of grace filling Jesus Christ without measure make him in the eyes of believers? O what a glory must it fix upon him!

He is Lovely in His Offices

Secondly, He is altogether lovely in his offices: let us consider for a moment the suitability, fullness, and comforting nature of them.

First, *The suitability of the offices of Christ to the miseries of men.* We cannot but adore the infinite wisdom of his receiving them. We are, by nature, blind and ignorant, at best but groping in the dim light of nature after God, Acts 17:27. Jesus Christ is a light to lighten the Gentiles, Isa. 49:6. When this great prophet came into the world, then did the day-spring from on high visit us, Luke 1:78. By nature we are alienated from, and at enmity against God; Christ comes into the world to be an atoning sacrifice, making peace by the blood of his cross, Col. 1:20. All the world, by nature, is in bondage and captivity to Satan, a miserable slavery. Christ comes with kingly power, to rescue sinners, as a prey from the mouth of the terrible one.

Secondly, *Let the fullness of his offices be also considered*, which make him able "to save to the uttermost, all that come to God by him," Heb. 7:25. The three offices, comprising in them all that our souls do need, become an universal relief to all our distresses; and therefore,

Thirdly, *Unspeakably comforting must the offices of Christ be to the souls of sinners.* If light be pleasant to our eyes, how pleasant is that light of life springing from the Sun of righteousness! Mal. 4:2. If a pardon be sweet to a condemned criminal, how sweet must the sprinkling the blood of Jesus be to the trembling conscience of a law-condemned sinner? If a rescue from a cruel tyrant is sweet to a poor captive, how sweet must it be to the ears of enslaved sinners, to hear the voice of liberty and deliverance proclaimed by Jesus Christ? Out of the several offices of Christ, as out of so many fountains, all the promises of the new covenant flow, as so many soul-refreshing streams of peace and joy. All the promises of illumination, counsel and direction flow out of Christ's prophetic office. All the promises of reconciliation, peace, pardon, and acceptation flow out of his priestly office, with the sweet streams of joy and spiritual comforts which accompany it. All the promises of converting, increasing, defending, directing, and supplying grace, flow out of the kingly office of Christ; indeed, all promises may be reduced to these three offices, so that Jesus Christ must be altogether lovely in his offices.

He is Lovely in His Relations.

First, *He is a lovely Redeemer*, Isa. 61:1. He came to open the prison-doors to them that are bound. Needs must this Redeemer be a lovely one, if we consider the depth of misery from which he redeemed us, even "from the wrath to come," 1 Thess. 1:10. Consider the numbers redeemed, and the means of their redemption. Rev. 5:9, "And they sang a new song, saying, 'You are worthy to take the book, and to open the seals thereof: for you were slain, and have redeemed us to God by your blood, out of every kindred and tongue, and people and nation.' " He redeemed us not with silver and gold, but with his own precious blood, by way of price, 1 Pet. 1:18,19. with his out-stretched and glorious arm, by way of power, Col. 1:13. he redeemed us freely, Eph. 1:7, fully Rom. 8:1, at the right time, Gal. 4:4, and out of special and particular love, John 17:9. In a word, he has redeemed us for ever, never more to come into bondage, 1 Pet. 1:5. John 10:28. O how lovely is Jesus Christ in the relation of a Redeemer to God's elect!

Secondly, *He is a lovely bridegroom* to all that he betroths to himself. How does the church glory in him, in the words following my text; "this is my Beloved, and this is my Friend, O ye daughters of Jerusalem!" Heaven and earth cannot show anyone like him, which needs no fuller proof than the following particulars:

1. That he betroths to himself, in mercy and in loving kindness, such deformed, defiled, and altogether unworthy souls as we are. We have no beauty, no goodness to make us desirable in his eyes; all the origins of his love to us are in his own breast, Deut. 7:7. He chooses us, not because we were, but in order that he might make us lovely Eph. 5:27. He came to us when we lay in our blood, and said unto us, "Live"; and that was the time of love, Ezek. 16:5.

2. He expects no restitution from us, and yet gives himself, and all that he has, to us. Our poverty cannot enrich him, but he made himself poor to enrich us, 2 Cor. 8:9. 1 Cor. 3:22.

3. No husband loves the wife of his bosom, as much as Christ loved his people, Eph. 5:25. He loved the church and gave him self for it.

4. No one bears with weaknesses and provocations as Christ does; the church is called "the Lamb's wife," Rev. 19:9.

5. No husband is so undying and everlasting a husband as Christ is; death separates all other relations, but the soul's union with Christ is not dissolved in the grave. Indeed, the day of a believer's death is his marriage day, the day of his fullest enjoyment of Christ. No husband can say to his wife, what Christ says to the believer, "I will never leave you, nor forsake you," Heb. 8:5.

6. No bridegroom enriches his bride with such honours by marriage, as Christ does; he makes them related to God as their father, and from that day the mighty and glorious angels think it no dishonour to be their servants, Heb. 1:14. The angels will admire the beauty and glory of the spouse of Christ, Rev. 21:9.

7. No marriage was ever consummated with such triumphal proceedings as the marriage of Christ and believers shall be in heaven, Psalm 14:14,15. "She shall be brought to the king in raiment of needle-work, the virgins, her companions that follow her, shall be brought unto thee; with gladness and rejoicing shall they be brought; they shall enter into the king's palace." Among the Jews, the marriage-house was called the house of praise; there was joy upon all hands, but nothing like the joy that will be in heaven when believers, the spouse of Christ, shall be brought there. God the Father will rejoice to behold the blessed accomplishment and confirmation of those glorious plans of his love. Jesus Christ, the Bridegroom will rejoice to see the travail of his soul, the blessed birth and product of all his bitter pains and agonies, Isa. 53:11. The Holy Spirit will rejoice to see the completion and perfection of that sanctifying design which was committed to his hand, 2 Cor. 5:5, to see those souls whom he once found as rough stones, now to shine as the bright, polished stones of the spiritual temple. Angels will rejoice: great was the joy when the foundation of this design was laid, in the incarnation of Christ, Luke 2:13. Great therefore must their joy be, when the top-stone is set up with shouting, crying, "Grace, grace." The saints themselves shall rejoice unspeakably, when they shall enter into the King's palace, and be forever with the Lord, 1 Thes. 4:17. Indeed there will be joy on all hands, except among the devils and damned, who shall gnash their teeth with envy at the everlasting advancement and glory of believers. Thus Christ is altogether lovely, in the relation of a Bridegroom.

Thirdly, *Christ is altogether lovely, in the relation of an Advocate.* 1 John 2:1, "If any man sin, we have an advocate with the Father, Jesus Christ the righteous, and he is the Propitiation." It is he that pleads the cause of believers in heaven. He appears for them in the presence of God, to prevent any new alienation, and to continue the state of friendship and peace between God and us. In this relation Christ is altogether lovely. For,

1. He makes our cause his own, and acts for us in heaven, as if for himself, Heb. 4:15. He is touched with a most tender understanding of our troubles and dangers, and is not only one with us by way of representation, but also one with us in respect of sympathy and affection.

2. Christ our Advocate tracks our cause and business in heaven, as his great and primary design and business. For this reason in Hebrews 7:25. he is said to "live for ever to make intercession for us." It is as if our concerns were so attended to by him there, that all the glory and honour which is paid him in heaven would not divert him one moment from our business.

3. He pleads the cause of believers by his blood. Unlike other advocates, it is not enough for him to lay out only words, which is a cheaper way of pleading; but he pleads for us by the voice of his own blood, as in Heb. 12:24, where we are said to be come "to the blood of sprinkling, that speaketh better things than that of Abel." Every wound he received for us on earth is a mouth opened to plead with God on our behalf in heaven. And hence it is, that in Rev. 5:6 he is represented standing before God, as a lamb that had been slain; as it were exhibiting and revealing in heaven those deadlywounds received on earth from the justice of God, on our account. Other advocates spend their breath, Christ spends his blood.

4. He pleads the cause of believers freely. Other advocates plead for reward, and empty the purses, while they plead the causes of their clients.

5. In a word, he obtains for us all the mercies for which he pleads. No cause miscarries in his hand, which he undertakes, Rom. 8:33, 34. O what a lovely Advocate is Christ for believers!

Fourthly, *Christ is altogether lovely in the relation of a friend*, for in this relation he is pleased to acknowledge his people, Luke 12:4, 5. There are certain things in which one friend manifests his affection and friendship to another, but there is not one like Christ. For,

1. No friend is so open-hearted to his friend as Christ is to his people: he reveals the very counsels and secrets of his heart to them. John 15:15. "Henceforth I call you not servants, for the servant knows not what his Lord does; but I have called you friends; for all things that I have heard of my Father, I have made known unto you.

2. No friend in the world is so generous and bountiful to his friend, as Jesus Christ is to believers; he parts with his very blood for them; "Greater love (he says) has no man than this, that a man lay down his life for his friends," John 15:13. He has exhausted the precious treasures of his invaluable blood to pay our debts. O what a lovely friend is Jesus Christ to believers!

3. No friend sympathizes so tenderly with his friend in affliction, as Jesus Christ does with his friends: "In all our afflictions he is afflicted," Heb. 4:15. He feels all our sorrows, needs and burdens as his own. This is why it is said that the sufferings of believers are called the sufferings of Christ, Col. 1:24.

4. No friend in the world takes that contentment in his friends, as Jesus Christ does in believers. Song of Songs 4:9. "You have ravished my heart, (he says to the spouse) you have ravished my heart with one of your eyes, with one chain of your neck." The Hebrew, here rendered "ravished," signifies to puff up, or to make one proud: how the Lord Jesus is pleased to glory in his people! How

he is taken and delighted with those gracious ornaments which himself bestows upon them! There is no friend so lovely as Christ.

5. No friend in the world loves his friend with as impassioned and strong affection as Jesus Christ loves believers. Jacob loved Rachel, and endured for her sake the parching heat of summer and cold of winter; but Christ endured the storms of the wrath of God, the heat of his indignation, for our sakes. David manifested his love to Absalom, in wishing, "O that I had died for you!" Christ manifested his love to us, not in wishes that he had died, but in death itself, in our stead, and for our sakes.

6. No friend in the world is so constant and unchangeable in friendship as Christ is. John 13:1, "Having loved his own which were in the world, he loved them unto the end." He bears with millions of provocations and wrongs, and yet will not break friendship with his people. Peter denied him, yet he will not disown him; but after his resurrection he says, "Go, tell the disciples, and tell Peter." Let him not think he has forfeited by that sin of his, his interest in me. Though he denied me, I will not disown him, Mark 16:7. O how lovely is Christ in the relation of a friend!

I might further show you the loveliness of Christ in his ordinances and in his providences, in his communion with us and communications to us, but there is no end of the account of Christ's loveliness: I will rather choose to press believers to their duties towards this altogether lovely Christ, which I shall briefly conclude in a few words.

APPLICATION

1. *Is Jesus Christ altogether lovely?* Then I beseech you set your souls upon this lovely Jesus. I am sure such an object as has been here represented, would compel love from the coldest breast and hardest heart. Away with those empty nothings, away with this vain deceitful world, which deserves not the thousandth part of the love you give it. Let all stand aside and give way to Christ. O if only you knew his worth and excellency, what he is in himself, what he has done for you, and deserved from you, you would need no arguments of mine to persuade you to love him!

2. *Esteem nothing lovely except as it is enjoyed in Christ, or used for the sake of Christ.* Love nothing for itself, love nothing separate from Jesus Christ. In two things we all sin in love of created things. We sin in the excess of our affections, loving them above the proper value of mere created things. We also

sin in the inordinacy of our affections, that is to say we give our love for created things a priority it should never have.

3. *Let us all be humbled for the corruption of our hearts* that are so eager in their affections for vanities and trifles and so hard to be persuaded to the love of Christ, who is altogether lovely. O how many pour out streams of love and delight upon the vain and empty created thing; while no arguments can draw forth one drop of love from their stubborn and unbelieving hearts to Jesus Christ! I have read of one Joannes Mollius, who was observed to go often alone, and weep bitterly; and being pressed by a friend to know the cause of his troubles, said "O! it grieves me that I cannot bring this heart of mine to love Jesus Christ more fervently."

4. *Represent Christ to the world as he is, by your behaviour towards him.* Is he altogether lovely? Let all the world see and know that he is so, by your delights in him and communion with him; zeal for him, and readiness to part with any other lovely thing upon his account. Proclaim his excellencies to the world, as the spouse did in these verses. Persuade them how much your beloved is better than any other beloved. Show his glorious excellencies as you speak of him; hold him forth to others, as he is in himself: altogether lovely. See that you "walk worthy of him unto all well pleasing," Col. 1:10. "Show forth the praises of Christ," 1 Pet. 2:19. Let not that "worthy name be blasphemed through you," James 2:7. He is glorious in himself, and he is sure to put glory upon you; take heed that you do not put shame and dishonours upon him; he has committed his honour to you, do not betray that trust.

Never be ashamed to be counted as a Christian: he is altogether lovely; he can never be a shame to you; it will be your great sin to be ashamed of him. Some men glory in their shame; do not let yourself be ashamed of your glory. If you will be ashamed of Christ now, he will be ashamed of you when he shall appear in his own glory, and the glory of all his holy angels. Be ashamed of nothing but sin; and among other sins, be ashamed especially for this sin, that you have no more love for him who is altogether lovely.

6. *Be willing to leave every thing that is lovely upon earth*, in order that you may be with the altogether lovely Lord Jesus Christ in heaven. Lift up your voices with the bride, Rev. 20:20 "Come Lord Jesus, come quickly." It is true, you must pass through the pangs of death into his intimacy and enjoyment; but surely it is worth suffering much more than that to be with this lovely Jesus. "The Lord direct your hearts into the love of God, and the patient waiting for Jesus Christ," 2 Thes. 3:5.

7. *Let the loveliness of Christ draw all men to him.* Is loveliness in the creature so attractive? And can the transcendent loveliness of Christ draw none? O the blindness of man! If you see no beauty in Christ that causes you to desire him, it is because the god of this world has blinded your minds.

8. *Strive to be Christ-like, if ever you would be lovely in the eyes of God and man.* Certainly, my brethren, it is only the Spirit of Christ within you, and the beauty of Christ upon you, which can make you lovely persons. The more you resemble him in holiness, the more will you show of true excellence and loveliness; and the more frequent and spiritual your communication and communion with Christ is, the more of the beauty and loveliness of Christ will be stamped upon your spirits, changing you into the same image, from glory to glory. Amen.

Epilogue

WE ARE NOW 2000 YEARS REMOVED from the historical events we have just described in this book. The passions of our Lord's life eventually led Him to the cruelty of the cross and to the conquest of the resurrection.

These passions resonated in the life of the early Church and were reflected in the writings of St. Paul. They were the foundation for the early Church. Many of the believers marched to their own death empowered by the passionate concerns of our Lord.

By the end of the first century, however, these passions were moving toward extinction. Many began to abandon the interests of the Lord in order to pursue their own willful desires. Slowly, an ecclesiastical society emerged that was founded on heartless humanistic theology, lifeless liturgical order, and clerically dominated leadership. This transition has sucked the life out of a passionate, vibrant Church.

Over the past 400 years the Church has experienced a reformation in theology and an acceleration in spiritual dynamic. In spite of this increase in spiritual enlightenment and the vitality of spiritual experiences, something is still missing in the Church.

The time is ripe for a fresh discovery of the passions of the Lord. This is the time to abandon our own personal pursuits and embrace the passions of our Lord. A remnant is rising up that is tired of the ways of religion and hungry for passionate intimacy.

The time is now. Let us be the generation that discovers and restores the passions of the Lord. May the fire of these discoveries spread to all the earth.

Let the passions burn!

To contact the author you may write him at:

Donald L. Milam
2958 Fillmore Drive
Chambersburg, Pa. 17201

Or you may e-mail him at:

dlm@destinyimage.com

Or visit his Web site at:

www.radicalgrace.org